Growing
Cyclamen

GAY NIGHTINGALE

Growing Cyclamen

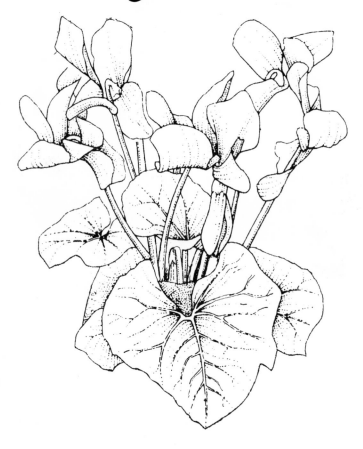

CROOM HELM London & Canberra
TIMBER PRESS Portland, Oregon

© 1982 Gay Nightingale
Croom Helm Ltd, 2-10 St John's Road, London SW11

British Library Cataloguing in Publication Data

Nightingale, Gay
   Growing cyclamen.
   1. Cyclamen
   I. Title
   635.9'33672   SB413.C9
   ISBN 0-7099-1805-4

First published in the USA in 1982 by Timber Press,
PO Box 1632
Beaverton, OR 97075
USA
All rights reserved
ISBN 0917304-41-1

Printed and bound in Great Britain

Contents

Contents

List of Figures

List of Tables

Technical drawings by A. Hamid.
Line drawings of plants by the author.

Foreword

At first, when the idea of a book on *Cyclamen* was suggested, it seemed best to treat the species separately from the florists' forms of *C.persicum*, but as the necessary research led to a deeper appreciation of the value of classification, I thought it would be far nicer to consider the large cultivated varieties in their proper place, i.e. as strains and cultivars of one species. Although this approach is more complex, I hope that it will serve to introduce the wild species to those who grow only the florists' varieties and vice versa.

PARADISI IN SOLE
Paradisus Terrestris.
or
A Garden of all sorts of pleasant flowers which our
English ayre will permitt to be noursed vp:
with
A Kitchen garden of all manner of herbes, rootes, & fruites,
for meate or sause vsed with vs,
and
An Orchard of all sorte of fruitbearing Trees
and shrubbes fit for our Land
together
With the right orderinge planting & preseruing
of them and their vses & vertues
Collected by John Parkinson
Apothecary of London.
1629

Qui veut parangonner l'artifice a Nature,
Et mes parcs à l'Eden, indiscret il mesure.

Le pas de l'elephant par le pas du ciron,
Et de l'aigle le vol par cil du moucheron.

Acknowledgements

My thanks are extended to the many kind people who have provided information during the preparation of this book: members of the Cyclamen Society, especially all members of the committee, past and present; Mr Peter Stageman and Dr Brent Elliott, librarians at the Royal Horticultural Society's Lindley Library; Mrs Lothian Lynas, Head Reference Librarian at The New York Botanical Garden; the librarians at Loughton Library and Ilford Reference Library; Mr R.D. Meikle of The Royal Botanic Gardens, Kew; Professor Dr Horn, University of Munich; Professor Dr R. Maatsch, University of Hanover; Dr C. Vonk Noordegraaf, Research Station for Floriculture, Aalsmeer; V.J. Francis of the Horticultural and Botanical Association; Mr A.B. Hender of Hurst; Mr J. Gibson and Mr M. Heath of Colgrave Seeds; Mr G.W. Carter and Mr E.H. Gray, Executive Directors of Suttons; Mr A.E. Radway, Managing Director of Samuel Dobie & Son; Mr K. Sangster, Managing Director of Thompson & Morgan; Mrs Bullivant of Buckhurst Hill Horticultural Society; Miss E.S. Burgoyne, Mrs K. Dryden and other members of the Alpine Garden Society.

I also wish to thank Elspeth Napier, Editor of *The Garden*, for kindly allowing me to quote briefly from the *Journal of the Royal Horticultural Society* and Colonel J.A. Mars for his permission to include short passages from *The Cyclamen Society's Journal*.

I am deeply indebted to the following people who have kindly lent their transparencies for publication in this book: Mrs D.A. Anderson for *C. purpurascens*; F.W. Buglass for *C. trochopteranthum* and *C. coum*; Mr and Mrs H.L. Crook for *C. balearicum* and *C. creticum*; B. Mathew for *C. parviflorum*; and B.B. Sparkes for *C. rohlfsianum* and *C. cyprium*. I would also like to express my gratitude to the publishers for all their help in producing this book.

Lastly, but not least, I thank all the members of my family for their patience and encouragement — and for their help with gardening and with the book.

A MAP SHOWING DISTRIBUTION OF THE CYCLAMEN SPECIES

Plants designated with an asterisk (*) have a wide distribution. Others are found only where numbered.

1. C. repandum*
   var. peloponnes
   var. rhodense
2. C. balearicum
3. C. creticum

4. C. coum*
   var. caucasicum
5. C. trochopteranthum
6. C. parviflorum

7. C. cilicium
   var. intaminatum
8. C. pseudibericum
9. C. libanoticum
10. C. cyprium

11. C. mirabile
12. C. persicum*
13. C. rohlfsianum
14. C. graecum

15. C. purpurascens*
    var. fatrense
    var. colchicum
16. C. hederifolium*
17. C. africanum
18. C. commutatum

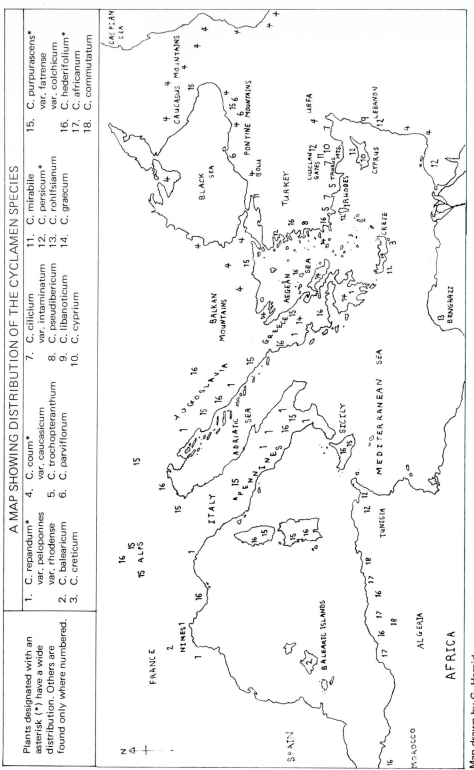

Map drawn by G. Hamid

CHAPTER 1

Introduction

Although the breeding of fancy florists' strains of *Cyclamen persicum* only began in the last century, cyclamen have been grown and written about since Plato's time. Theophrastus, born about 370 BC, was a practical gardener; although he has also been called the father of botany. He learnt classification of form and things from his master Plato and adapted these ideas in order to study plants. He recorded detail, such as the shape of a flower or the presence of fragrance, in much the same way as botanists do today. The name

History:
CyclamenSince
Plato's Time

Figure 1.1
C. persicum,
Wild Species

cyclamen is derived from the Greek 'kyklamenos' or 'kyklos' meaning circle-form.

Archaeologists have discovered early flower paintings on Crete, and in the Middle Ages, the art of gardening spread through the countries around the Mediterranean and botanical collections were started in monasteries. At first, plants were grown mainly for their medicinal properties; but flowers were treasured and often grown for decorating the church.

The hardy *Cyclamen* species *coum* and *hederifolium* were already in cultivation in Gerard's European garden by 1596, and it is believed that *C. persicum* was brought to this country in 1731 from Cyprus. Philip. Miller had been made head-gardener at the Chelsea Physic Garden in 1722, where he was Keeper until 1771, and the first edition of his voluminous work, *Miller's Gardeners Dictionary*, was published in 1731. Inside the huge cover of the eighth edition, published in 1768, it is delightful to find the word 'cyclamen' under the following heading:

> A catalogue of plants, which are too tender to live abroad in winter in England, but require no artificial heat, they are commonly called greenhouse plants; but those whose leaves and stalks are succulent, will succeed better if they are kept in a dry airy glass-case in winter where they may enjoy the sun and air at all times when the weather is mild.

It is amazing how hardy some of the species are when we consider that they continue in flower through the coldest months.

Turning to the entry on Cyclamen in the book, we discover that even in the early eighteenth century, Miller was able to tell us that: 'This genus of plants is ranged in the first section of Linnaéus's fifth class, intitled Pentandria Monogynia, the flower having five stamina and one style.'

The system of binomial plant classification was devised by the Swedish biologist Carolus Linnaeus (1707-78), and his *Systema Naturae* first appeared in 1735. He gave all those that interbreed naturally a species name and placed similar species into a group, which he called a genus, so that each plant now has two Latin names. Scientists sometimes add form and varietal names; but the two Latin names are still the most important, as they can be understood and used by botanists and horticulturalists all over the world.

Philip Miller distinguished six species within the genus *Cyclamen: europaeum* syn. *hederifolium, purpurascens,* 'The Persian Cyclamen' or *persicum, vernale, orbiculatum* and *coum.* The name *hymale* makes an appearance here too. However, there has been confusion in the naming of cyclamen and, since 1813, botanists have agreed to use the name that was first given to the plant. Miller explains that the first species (then called *europaeum*) is the most hardy: 'After the flowers are fallen, the soot-stalks twist up like a screw, inclosing the germen in the center, and lay down close to the surface of the ground between the leaves, which serve as a protection to the seed.'

Linnaeus visited the Chelsea Physic Garden, and Miller wrote: 'Though Dr Linnaeus supposes them but one species, it is well known that the fifth sort will endure the greatest frost in the open air, whereas all the Persian sorts are tender, and require shelter in the winter.'

Although Linnaeus named his one species *europaeum*, we know this today as *hederifolium*. *Cyclamen purpurascens* was recognised as a separate species and named by Miller, and this is the plant we call *purpurascens* today, although it has been referred to incorrectly as *europaeum* in the meantime. (The chapter on species may help to solve some of the difficulties regarding synonyms.)

There was much enthusiasm over all the new plants that were being brought back by explorers about this time. To cater for the growing interest Curtis started his *Botanical Magazine* in 1787, the longest-surviving periodical anywhere. In volume 1, there is a detailed colour plate of *coum*, dated 1786. Later, he writes of *persicum*: 'It is generally cultivated in pots in light undunged earth' — an original way of describing compost! The magazine was continued by John Sims, and in volume 25, there is a description of *hederifolium* in Latin, followed by a note beside the illustration (unmistakeably cyclamen) which is of interest to gardeners:

> The ivy-leaved Cyclamen is said to be a native of Italy; it is a very valuable plant, on account of its early flowering, sweet scent, and beautiful foliage. It is not so hardy as *europaeum*, but can be cultivated in the open ground. *May be propagated by cuttings of the root*. (My italics).

Vegetative propagation was practised all those years ago and yet it is still not widely known that it is possible to increase cyclamen in this way.

In 1828, J.C. Loudon, a garden designer of tremendous talent and will-power, wrote *An Encyclopaedia of Gardening*. It was aimed at the expanding middle classes with their newly built houses and gardens. He was married to Jane Loudon, author of *Loudon's Ladies' Flower Garden*, which was also published during the early nineteenth century.

Mrs Loudon calls *repandum* 'the angular-leaved cyclamen' but gives the synonym '*Hederaefolium*' and writes that 'the species is a native of Greece, whence it was introduced about 1806'. She lists under other species of cyclamen: '*C. hederaefolium*, Lin. *C. neapolitanum*, Ten.', and comments: 'This species has red flowers. It is native of Naples, and was introduced in 1826.' She claims that: 'The word Cyclamen signifies a succession of circles, in allusion to the curious manner in which the flower stalks curl up when the seeds begin to ripen; and the name of sowbread alludes to the fondness of swine for the tubers of the Italian species.' However, Miller said earlier that 'it is called sowbread, because the root is round like a loaf'. Other writers have called cyclamen 'food of the gods' – no doubt they were looking at the flowers!

Mrs Loudon also mentions *coum* and says that 'the species grows wild in many parts of Italy and Germany' but adds: 'In British gardens, however, it seldom flowers before March or April, unless kept in pots', which sounds surprising for *coum*. Under *europaeum* (nowadays *hederifolium*), she writes that the species was introduced before 1596, 'and is consequently one of the oldest exotic flowers in British gardens'.

In Robert Sweet's *British Flower Garden* (vol. II, 1825-7), there is a colour-drawing of 'sweet-scented *Cyclamen europaeum*'. He wrote: 'our drawing of this delightfully fragrant species was taken from a fine plant ... the fragrance of which exceeds almost every other plant with which we are acquainted.' He hoped that the genus would soon be understood. In the meantime, The Royal Horticultural Society had been formed in 1804. John Lindley was the first Secretary and the beautiful RHS Library was named after him.

By the middle of the nineteenth century, indoor plants were increasing in popularity and Joseph Paxton, the garden boy who rose to become a leading garden designer, created a garden under glass on the site of the Great Exhibition of 1851. (The Crystal Palace was moved, between 1852-4, to Sydenham, where Paxton also designed the surrounding grounds.) He was responsible for acquiring many of the new plants from overseas which led to further interest and development of the garden scene. Mostly due to Paxton's influence, greenhouses were bought for many more gardens, and cyclamen have been sold in increasing quantities as house and greenhouse plants in Europe since that time.

The focus on gardening is highlighted in the following extract from Prince Albert's speech at the opening of the new gardens of The Royal Horticultural Society, reported in vol. I of the *RHS Journal* in 1861.

That which last year was still a vague conception, is, to-day, a reality: and, I trust, will be accepted as a valuable attempt, at least, to re-unite the science and art of Gardening to the sister arts of Architecture, Sculpture, and Painting.

Figure 1.2 Sutton's Cyclamens (1892)

CYCLAMEN PERSICUM.

Half-hardy perennial. Height 6 inches.

SUTTON'S SEEDLING CYCLAMENS, flowered within twelve months from date of sowing. (*Engraved from a Photograph.*)

Sutton's Prize, mixed ...per packet, 5s. and 2s. 6d.

We have for many years past so carefully selected the best types of Cyclamen persicum, that we believe our strain cannot be surpassed. The flowers almost equal the Giant varieties in size, but the plants are much more free-flowering, with a compact and bushy habit. For table or greenhouse decoration during the winter months our Improved varieties are invaluable. The seed here offered consists exclusively of improved types of Cyclamen either as regards the colour or the size and shape of the flowers. The above illustration is engraved direct from a photograph, but it is on so reduced a scale that it very inadequately represents the large collection of plants flowered within twelve months from the date seed was sown. The house is 76 feet long.

'The Cyclamen has turned out well, the flowers being produced in large numbers and of exquisite colour.'—Mr. R. Cotton, *Gardener to the Dowager Lady* Buxton.

'Your strain of Cyclamen is admired by all. I never saw one-year-old plants flower so freely.'—Mr. W Clayton, *Gardener to* W. R. H. Powell, Esq.

'Your Cyclamens produce the largest blooms I have seen, and they are of splendid habit.'—Mr. A. R. Wilson, *Gardener to* W. Young, Esq.

'Your Prize Cyclamens are superb; some pure white are the best I have seen.'—Mr. J. Wyke, *Gardener to* E. P. Westby, Esq.

'The Cyclamens I had from your seed proved to be the finest I have had.'—Chas. J. Francis, Esq., Hafod.

'200 plants of your Cyclamen are splendid.'—Mr. A. Haggart, *Gardener to* Mrs. Foster.

'The Cyclamens and Primulas have flowered splendidly, some of the Cyclamen plants having upwards of 40 blooms.'—Mr. H. Phillips, *Gardener to* Mrs. King.

Sutton's White Butterfly.

The finest pure white Cyclamen, compact in habit, with beautifully marbled foliage. The flowers are produced freely, and are remarkable for great substance and good form.
Per packet, 3s. 6d. and 1s. 6d.

'Your Butterfly Cyclamen is a grand flower.'—Mr. J. Collier, *Gardener to the* Rev. F. H. Hichens.

'Two hundred and fifty plants of your White Butterfly, although only sown last February, are full of buds, and will be a perfect picture with their magnificent marbled foliage.'—Mr. F. Bush, *Gardener to* E. Poulsen, Esq.

Sutton's Vulcan.

A Cyclamen possessing extraordinarily deep crimson colour. The flowers look very rich by artificial light, and make a charming contrast to the pure white flowers of our Butterfly.
Per packet, 5s. and 2s. 6d.

'In richness Vulcan bears the palm.'—Journal of Horticulture.

SUTTON'S GIANT CYCLAMEN.

A magnificent strain, with flowers of extraordinary size and great substance. The leaves are proportionately large and very beautifully marked with silver grey. We confidently recommend the following:—

Sutton's Giant White. Flowers pure white ... per packet, 2s. 6d.

'The Giant White Cyclamens I had from your seed are superb. They were in bloom 11 months after sowing.'—The Rev. Campbell Lock, Chalton.

'The Giant White stands at the head of White Cyclamen, a grand strain, the flowers of the purest white, large in size and handsomely formed.—R. Dean.'—Gardeners' Magazine.

Sutton's Giant Rose. Flowers of a purplish rose colour...per pkt., 2s. 6d.

Sutton's Giant Crimson. Bright crimson ... ,, 2s. 6d.

Sutton's Giant Purple. Rich purple ... ... ,, 2s. 6d.

Sutton's Giant Crimson and White. Flowers quite as large as those previously named, but differing in colour, the base being crimson and the upper part pure white ... ... per packet, 2s. 6d.

A Collection of the five varieties, separate ... ... 7s. 6d.

Sutton's Giant, mixed ... ... per packet, 5s. and 2s. 6d.

CYCLAMEN PERSICUM.

Album, pure white... per pkt., 1s. 6d.	**Rubrum**, deep red...per pkt., 1s. 6d.	
Phœnix, intense crimson ,, 1s. 6d.	**Odoratum**, mixed colours;	
Roseum, rose, carmine base ,, 1s. 6d.	sweet-scented flowers ,, 1s. 6d.	
Roseum album, white,	**Purpureum**, rich purple ,, 1s. 6d.	
red base ... ... ,, 1s. 6d.	**Mixed** ... ... ,, 1s. 6d.	

Collection of six varieties, separate ... ... per packet, 5s.

Cyclamen europœum (hardy) ... ... ,, 1s.

CULTURE.—Seed may be sown at any time of the year. The important months are October and November, and January or February for ensuring a succession. Use either pots or pans firmly filled with rich loam and leaf mould, mingled with a sufficiency of sharp sand to ensure drainage. Dibble the seed an inch apart and a quarter of an inch deep. Autumn sowings must have a temperature of not less than 45°, and winter sowings from 56° to 70°, not higher. The seed germinates very slowly and irregularly. Transfer to thumb-pots as ready, and shift on until the 48-size is reached. The whole secret of successful Cyclamen culture may be summed up in a few words: constant and unvarying heat, a moist atmosphere, and abundant supplies of water without stagnation; free circulation of air, avoiding cold draughts; light in winter and shade in summer, with freedom from insect pests.

SUTTON & SONS, Seed Growers and Merchants, READING, ENGLAND.

88

17

Introduction

William Robinson, editor of *The Garden* from 1868-1912, did not like the formal style of the ponds, Italian urns and bedding plants of the Paxton era. He decided to bring back the natural flower garden, and wrote about his own ideas in *The Wild Garden*. He advised his readers to turn their attention to hardy plants from England and abroad, and this led to further interest in alpine plants and consequently cyclamen species.

Although it is believed that the first *persicum* cyclamen were brought to Britain on the East India Company shipping line in the eighteenth century, it wasn't until after the Crystal Palace; the designing of new public parks; the subsequent demand for more seeds and more knowledge; the formation of the RHS and the development of horticultural journals, that the variety of natural forms became more widely known. In 1860, the Floral Committee reported twelve named varieties as 'beautiful spring-flowering greenhouse perennials' among which were 'purpureum', 'grandiflorum', 'rubrum coccineum' and 'marginatum purpureum'.

The famous firm of Thompson & Morgan had its beginnings in 1855 — four years after the Great Exhibition. William Thompson published *The English Flower Garden* between 1852 and 1853, and later a seed list. His catalogue of 1865 included *C. europaeum*, *C. macrophyllum* and *persicum* under the general heading: PRIMROSE TRIBE. The first two were listed as hardy and the third half-hardy; the price was sixpence per packet, which must have seemed expensive in those days. Suttons, established in 1806, introduced *C. persicum* in 1867.

Carters was founded in 1835; but it wasn't until 1882 that the genus *Cyclamen* warranted a full half-page of his Tested Seeds Catalogue with a black and white lithograph as illustration. *C. persicum* 'White Swan' appears here as 'one of the most beautiful white cyclamen in cultivation' but all seven varieties offered for sale had been awarded a First Class Certificate of Merit. The seeds were scarce and cost 1s 6d, 2s 6d and 5s per packet — a lot of money at the time.

Rosy pinks, lilacs, light reds and whites were all being bred by nurserymen during the latter half of the nineteenth century; but the dark reds, purples and scarlets available today were yet to come — these colours have all been bred in cultivation.

Wisley Gardens were presented to the RHS in 1903. A representative collection of cyclamen species is kept there under glass and some of the hardiest are naturalised out of doors. They are described in the January 1950 issue of the *Journal*:

> During favourable spells a number of deceptively delicate-looking cyclamen species will be in flower. *C. coum* carries its fat flowers

of pale magenta above leaded green leaves. *C. graecum* needs some protection, whence it will produce attractive rosy-red flowers with darker carmine streaks at the mouth. Perhaps the most graceful of all is *C. persicum*, being far removed from the flamboyant varieties derived from it by the florists. It grows somewhat taller than the other species and the twisted petals give the flower a rather frightened appearance.

In the same year, Fred Streeter described *Cyclamen persicum* in the *RHS Journal*. Apparently, three tubers sent home to Petworth by Lady Leconfield from Cyprus, in 1925, had flowered from November to March that year, after the tubers had been baked for about twelve weeks in the nectarine house in full sun. Seedlings of these plants had germinated one month after sowing and they had been grown without warmth, as the heating was needed for all the houseplants. At the time of the February 1950 Show, the three original plants were still alive and growing in 15 cm pans carrying 200 flowers. We can see from this that it is natural for *persicum* species to produce many flowers every season.

Mr Streeter crossed some large-flowered *persicum* plants with these species to try and produce dainty, fragrant offspring. He managed to obtain scented blooms but found it difficult to get them to breed true. (It is curious that although he did not feed the tubers, they flowered every year.) He also tried growing some of his plants in sheltered places in the garden.

Also around 1950, Mr Allan Jackson, a lecturer in horticulture at Wye College, selected a silver-leaf *C. persicum giganteum* with a distinctive, wide marking on the margins of the foliage. He used it in a breeding programme with a fragrant white, making crosses with these two plants and the wild species *persicum*. The first crosses were back-crossed to the parents and a number of recognisable varieties which bred fairly true eventually emerged.

These early crosses of the large-flowering *persicum* with the wild species, together with other similar crosses made by Dr Watts at Reading, led to the development of the mini-cyclamen F_1 hybrids that are rapidly gaining in popularity today.

Modern architecture and open plan offices, with their massive glass windows and light interiors, resulted in more cyclamen being sold as gift-plants in London and large cities throughout the world. Novelty plants with double flowers or frilly corollas fascinated the breeders. The first Dobies F_1 hybrid — a double from Sakata in Japan — was introduced in 1960, and he produced the double variety known as Kimona from the American double strain (Vogt's) between 1963 and 1970.

The majority of cyclamen are now grown in small pots in Germany;

but this trend took a number of years to get started. We are about ten years behind in marketing technique, although more advanced in scientific research.

The Cyclamen Society (a registered charity) was formed in January 1977 for the benefit of all who are interested in the genus. Twelve people attended the inaugural meeting, held in a committee room at the RHS New Hall, Westminster, London. The society grew rapidly and by 1980 the *Journal* (edited by Col. James Mars) was being sent to members all over the world. The seed exchange is very popular with members, many of whom donate rare seed in generous quantities so that new members can begin a cyclamen collection. It is hoped that spreading seed in cultivation will help conserve the species in the wild. Conferences are held regularly, often with the University of London; and the Society has a stand three times a year as part of the RHS Show.

Geography: The Natural Distribution of the Species

C. africanum is native to Algeria (see also *C. commutatum* below).

C. balearicum plants are abundant in their natural habitat of the Balearic Islands, particularly on Majorca. And a few isolated colonies remain in the south of France: in 1979, the alpine plant specialist nurseryman, Paul Christian, found a little colony growing wild in the Hérault region. The plants were lodged in leaf-mould filled crevices of limestone rocks under a beech tree and at the base of cliffs — mostly in heavy shade. Also found by Glasau in the Nîmes area of France many years ago.

Figure 1.3
C. balearicum

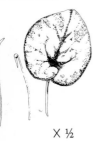

X ½

C. cilicium grows freely in parts of the forest region of Cilicia and Anatolia in southern Turkey, where many plants are in pine woods. In 1956, Dr P.H. Davies reported seeing masses of plants near the snowline, and since then other explorers have written of similar experiences. *C. cilicium* var. *intaminatum* was originally collected by E.K. Balls in 1934, under the numbers 669a and 628, from the area known as the Cicilian Gates Pass.

C. commutatum is found in Algeria, but plants of this species are separable from *C. africanum* only by a chromosome count: *C. africanum* (34) and *C. commutatum* (68).

C. coum Mill. Plants of this species are distributed across north Iran, the border of the Black Sea, Bulgaria, European Turkey, Anatolia, western Syria, the Lebanon and northern Israel. In the mountainous regions of Turkey *coum* grows abundantly on north-facing slopes, and along the Black Sea coast they grow in sandy soil alongside snowdrops and on the hillsides in hazel woodland alongside prim-roses. In the region of the Caucasus, there is an overlap of *C. coum* var. *coum*, which has kidney-shaped leaves and *C. coum* var. *caucasicum*, which has more heart-shaped leaves. Some authorities would like the latter to be recognised as a species, e.g. *C. caucasicum*; however, the distinguishing characteristics seem to be variable.

C. creticum. These beautiful white-flowering plants are distributed in the more remote areas of Crete, where the tubers are found deep in the stony, red soil of the hillsides, under olive trees. They flower in late spring in the shade of sweet chestnuts, often accompanied by wild orchids. They are sometimes found growing under pine trees; and sometimes near *Anemone blanda* or primroses.

C. cyprium is indigenous to Cyprus. Writing in the Alpine Garden Society Bulletin, Eileen and Nathan Mutch state: 'The autumn *C. cyprium*, small, exquisite and sweetly perfumed, prefers cooler and less sun-drenched sites, as in the lightly wooded scree country below the northern face of Mount Prophitis near Karmi and in the Paphos forest up to 3,000 ft.'

Figure 1.4
C. cyprium

C. graecum is endemic to Greece, and was originally described from specimens collected by Berger in the north-east Peloponnese. A form from Cyprus is sometimes referred to as *cypro-graecum*, but this is not a separate species. Other names, such as *gauidurowrysii* and *mindleri*, also refer to geographical locations. Spreading southwards across the Greek islands and northern Turkey, plants of the species are often found in sunny places under stones or slabs of limestone rock in woods, and in the same districts as *hederifolium*, although the latter is more likely to be in the shade.

At the Autumn 1981 RHS Show, the Alpine Garden Society's Saunders' Spoon was won by the owner of a choice form of *graecum* from Mount Hymettos on mainland Greece.

C. hederifolium is native to southern Europe; it is predominantly a shade-plant distributed through Italy, Corsica, Sardinia, parts of southern France and Greece. Colonies have also been located in western Turkey, Yugoslavia, Crete and islands in the Aegean Sea. The island forms are often quite strongly scented. Numerous plants have been found in oak forest in southern Yugoslavia, and some of the Italian hillsides are covered with wild *hederifolium* growing among olive trees or in the shade of chestnut woodland. In remote areas, this species grows on the rocky banks of streams and rivers. After visiting Turkey, Dr Peter Davies said that this species 'grew between the seats of the ruined Greek theatre, at Ephesus'.

C. libanoticum originally came from the Lebanon at the end of the nineteenth century, and since then very few have been seen in the wild. Fortunately, quite a number of plants have been bred in cultivation – they have been established out of doors in gardens from Hampshire to Cornwall, and under glass in other parts of England.

C. mirabile is endemic in south-west Turkey, where tubers grow in limestone 'soil in a similar habitat to *cilicium.*

C. parviflorum grows freely on meadows high up on the eastern Pontic mountains with gentians, crocuses and other alpine delights. The soil consists of rich, dark humus of the kind that suits dwarf rhododendrons. Brian Mathews said: 'in the wild the leaves remain pressed to the surface of the ground and the flower stems rise only 1-2 cm'. In my experience, plants of this species develop in exactly the same way in cultivation, if kept in cool shade and not coddled in a greenhouse. News has been received of plants that have become acclimatised in New Zealand, and as they are hardy in Britain, the species will probably be more widely grown in cultivation.

C. persicum is distributed in its natural habitat through Cilicia in southern Turkey, Crete, Cyprus, Palestine, Rhodes, Syria and Tunisia; but not, as popularly supposed, in Persia. The Tunisian form grows among olive and tangerine trees in sandy soil, which is very hot and dry in September; but cool in the day – especially in the shade – and quite cold at night in November, although above freezing. Most of the mini-cyclamen seen in florists' shops have been bred from the wild Cyprus forms crossed with large-flowering cultivars.

Figure 1.5
C. pseudibericum

C. pseudibericum. The deep magenta form of this really lovely species, thought by many to be the finest in the genus, has been found in Karatepe and Düldül Dag in the Amanus Mountains of Turkey, where it was sheltered by beech trees. There is also a rare pink form in Dörtyol.

C. purpurascens Mill. This delightfully fragrant species is distributed across Italy, Bulgaria, southern Switzerland, northern Yugoslavia and Austria, where it is widespread in the area south of Vienna, and is generally found in regions where there are limestone rocks and beech woods. The white-flowering form *C. purpurascens album* is extremely rare, both in its natural habitat of northern Croatia in Yugoslavia and in cultivation. The equally difficult to find *C. purpurascens* var. *colchicum* came originally from the Caucasus, where plants grow high above sea level in shaded, deep rock crevices, and the other uncommon form, *C. purpurascens* var. *fatrense* was first collected in Czechoslovakia.

C. repandum is endemic to the Mediterranean basin from southern France through Corsica, Italy, Sardinia, Sicily, Greece, Crete and central Yugoslavia — often in the shade of olive trees on the islands. The forms from Rhodes and the Peloponnese are particularly fine and rare. They are considerably different from the common type found elsewhere. According to Professor O. Schwarz, *C. repandum* var. *rhodense* Meikle (*C. rhodium* Gorer) besides being native to Rhodes is also widespread in Crete. Quite possibly the Peloponnese form also exists there, as a specimen of this scarce and lovely plant was sent to me in place of *C. creticum*!

C. rohlfsianum has a limited distribution among limestone rocks between Benghazi and Derna in Libya, North Africa.

C. trochopteranthum is native to coniferous forest in south-western Turkey, where it is protected by limestone rocks.

General Botany of the Cyclamen

There are eighteen species of the genus *Cyclamen*, which belongs to the *Primulaceae*, largest family of the order Primulales. The family also contains the genus *Primula*, therefore cyclamen are closely related to primulas, primroses and polyanthus — although one obvious difference is that cyclamen grow from tubers. But before we take a look at some typical tubers, let us consider the tremendous variety to be found in cyclamen leaves, as I hope this will give you a better taste for the genus — it is worth cultivating a fascination for foliage first!

Cyclamen leaves are radical, that is they arise directly from the tuber. In some of the species and forms, the foliage stands almost erect while in others it develops on long, creeping petioles. The two types of leaf carriage are as much due to variation in form *within a species*, caused by natural and artificial selection, as they are due to the different characteristics of the species.

Variation in form has long interested me, and I am fascinated by the fact that the heart-, kidney-, dagger- or ivy-shaped leaves can be lightly silvered, heavily silvered or entirely without silver, and by the fact that the shades of green vary from dull to bright, through grey-greens and pewter-greens. (Some idea of the possible mathematical permutation of the genes responsible for leaf-colour and shape can be gained from close observation of the *hederifolium* species.)

However, the foliage of cyclamen also varies in size and texture. Individual leaves can be large and small on one specimen, according to their stage of development and maturity due to the changing seasons and whether the plant has received liquid fertiliser or not. Leaves can also vary in size on two specimens of the same species given different cultural treatment. However, under controlled conditions, the smallest leaves will be found on *C. parviflorum* and the form *C. cilicium* var. *intaminatum*. Some forms of *coum* come next with slightly larger foliage and the largest leaves are usually seen on *rohlfsianum*, *africanum* or cultivated strains of *persicum*. Texture varies too from the thick, leathery leaves with horny margins that can easily be felt on some forms of *africanum* to the thin leaves of *repandum* that soon curl up if exposed to sun. The leaves of *graecum* are more velvety than *persicum* in both texture and appearance, which is a help when it comes to distinguishing between them.

Most species have markings on the upper surface of the leaves, mostly a hastate or spear-shaped pattern on a dark or light background, although sometimes foliage is a dark, matt green as seen in some forms of *coum*, but most species have at least one form which bears an intricate pattern either in silver or varying shades of green and grey. Occasionally the markings on the leaves of one plant will be exactly the reverse of the markings on the plant growing close by: for example, in *hederifolium*, a plant might have a margin of deep green with a pale apple-green centre; another might have an apple-green margin merging into a dark centre. Other leaves have a silver net or reticulate pattern and this is seen clearly on good specimens of *purpurascens*. In some species, the silvering is almost spread over the entire surface; in others it is reduced to fine broken lines. *C. libanoticum* has a characteristic dull band around the margin. But the silver spots of the Peloponnese *repandum* are rather splendid and some of the *persicum* leaves are so decorative that they rival the foliage of non-flowering houseplants. *C. graecum* is another species that has brilliant leaf patterns and there are so many forms to collect. The colour of the under surface of the leaves varies, according to species and strains within the species, from plain green through shades of beetroot red to purple — as in *purpurascens*. One point of interest, however, is that the leaves can emerge before the flowers, with the flowers, or after the flowers have been in bloom for some time.

The Tuber and Roots

All cyclamen develop corm-like tubers which vary considerably in size and shape, according to species, from the tiny spheres of *cilicium* var. *intaminatum* to the giant dinner-plate or coffee-table-sized flattened food storage organs of *hederifolium*, and the heavy globular forms of *graecum*. The tubers do not vary only in size and shape, but in skin covering and root system. The tuber of this genus is really a swollen hypocotyl.

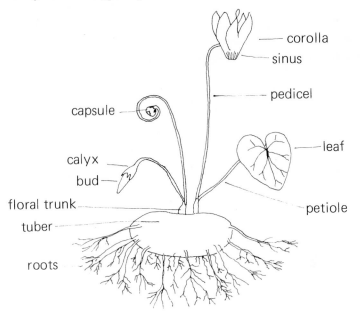

Figure 1.6
A Cyclamen Plant

The tubers of *persicum* are round, tending to become like very thick pancakes as they age. The spherical shape found in the tuber of most *balearicum, coum, creticum, cyprium, libanoticum, repandum* and *trochopteranthum* is typical of the genus. The tubers of *africanum, cilicium* and *hederifolium* tend to be more flattened and in some cases concave on one side; the tuber of *graecum* is more oval in appearance. Two species are atypical: *purpurascens* has basically round tubers, but the floral trunks or branches that extend from the top make them fairly easy to distinguish; the rare *rohlfsianum* has a peculiar shape, as it often looks as if someone has taken odd bites out of the tuber! Deep cavities sometimes develop and layers of tuber form in time: wide, spreading and shelf-like.

When the tubers of one species are handled after another in quick succession, there is a noticeable difference in the feel and colour. The colour varies from light, greenish-brown, as in *cyprium*, through grey-brown — as in *hederifolium*; to red-brown — as in *graecum*. *C. parviflorum* has bright, bead-green tubers when they first develop from the seedling stage. The outer skin of some species is thick and corky, as in *africanum, cyprium, hederifolium* and *purpurascens*. The older tubers of *persicum* become flaky — especially when the plant is grown with the top of the tuber exposed. *C. graecum* also has this habit, although as the tubers are normally buried well in the

25

pot or ground they are not so readily observed when in a non-resting state. The skin of *coum*, *cilicium* and *trochopteranthum* is remarkably thin and will break under the light pressure of the fingers when handling, if care is not taken to avoid damage. Fine hairs cover the skin of some young tubers.

It is worth examining the way the roots emerge from the tuber, as sometimes this will help you decide which species you are holding. Many of the species have a mass of fibrous roots; according to species, the roots emerge from the base, from the sides and top, from a point to one side at the base, or all over the surface of the tuber. The roots of *graecum* are easily distinguished from other cyclamen roots as they are long and thick, to reach right down into the soil or between rocks.

It had been thought that the species *africanum* and *hederifolium* could be differentiated by the way the roots grow. *C. africanum* roots usually appear from all over the outer covering of the tuber, whereas *hederifolium* roots emerge from the upper surface and sides, leaving the rounded base smooth. However, it now seems that the large number of forms of both *africanum* and *hederifolium*, and the inter-specific hybrids between *africanum* and *hederifolium* which are also possible means that root formation patterns can be found at several stages between the two species.

C. purpurascens is another species that roots over the entire surface of the tuber, but this species has other distinguishing features such as floral trunks, evergreen leaves with a characteristic shape — even the tuber is sufficiently different from *africanum* as to make it easily recognised. The species *rohlfsianum* has roots on the sides and base in groups on the tuber. But here again, the tuber can easily be distinguished from the tubers of other species, so there is less chance of confusion for the novice.

Floral trunks occur on other species besides *purpurascens*. They are often seen on *graecum*, *persicum* and rarely on the others, forming only as a means of survival, when they are growing in unhospitable surroundings such as under rocks or deeply underground. Sometimes they form on *graecum* or *hederifolium* when seedlings are self-sown on the parent tuber and the one-, two- and three-year-old seedlings have to compete for light and air. The parent plant is forced to send up a floral trunk through the foliage of the seedlings.

The Flower

The cyclamen is spectacular because of the way the corolla bends backwards as though the flower has been turned inside out. Few casual observers ever notice the greeny-brown sepals hidden at the top of the stalk or pedicel.

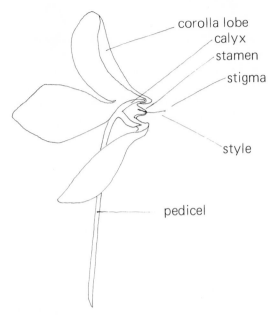

corolla lobe
calyx
stamen
stigma
style
pedicel

Figure 1.7
Section of a Flower

The calyx has five lance-shaped segments. The shape alters slightly with the species, becoming much more ovate or dome-shaped in the cultivated strains of *persicum*. The corolla is hypogynous with a short tube opening out into five separate petal segments, which are reflexed at an angle of $90°$-$180°$. The flower is unique in shape and other plants are compared to it; hence, *Narcissus cyclamineus*. The ovary is superior and the fruit, a capsule, has many seeds.

Although there are no nectaries in cyclamen, most species have at least some scented forms — the scent being secreted from specialised cells of the corolla. It is noticeable that when the corolla falls off the scent dies. The strongest fragrance is found in wild *persicum* and some of the recent cultivated strains. And it is well known that the sweet-smelling flowers of *purpurascens* are picked in parts of Italy and made into bunches for the table and tourists. Other cyclamen have a spicy aroma and one at least is more an odour than a fragrance.

The flowers of the giant cultivated strains have been bred in many colours from pinks, lilacs and whites, through crimson and scarlet to almost black-purple. The large petals can be entire or fimbriated and frilled like some orchids. However, with size has come a regrettable loss of fragrance. Apparently, the same energy that is required for scent-making cells in the corolla is needed to form giant petals with the result that the larger the flower becomes, the less chance there is of strong fragrance. Horticulturalists are now trying to breed highly fragrant miniature *persicum* plants.

Another intriguing phenomenon that occurs in the *persicum* species is the production of double flowers. These are usually non-fertile with either the gynoecium or the androecium — more often the latter — becoming adapted into petal-like structures. Thus a flower might appear to have ten petals in place of five. In these cases, the sinus can look perfectly normal, apart from the extra petals and the lack of mature anthers.

Flowers of the wild species are considerably smaller than those of some cultivated strains, but not less attractive. Indeed, many people find them more exquisite. The size ranges from the tiny flowers of *C. cilicium* var. *intaminatum* with *coum* and *parviflorum* flowers just a little larger at 2 cm, to the 4 cm flowers of *africanum* and *persicum* species. The flowers of *libanoticum* look as large as these because they are not twisted; but the former two species can be longer and wider if laid out on a board.

A number of species have auricles, or ear-like protrusions, on the part of the corolla tube where the petals separate and bend sharply backwards (see chapter 5). The petals are held at different angles: those of *trochopteranthum* are only halfway reflexed giving the flower an appearance resembling a child's windmill; others are twisted and folded. But all cyclamen flowers are easily recognised by the characteristic way the sinus or mouth points downwards with the petals flung backwards like a moth about to land.

Flower colours, excluding cultivated strains, include all shades of pink from the faintest blush tint to a clear salmon, pale lavender pinks, mauves and deep pinks, carmines and crimsons. There are also various white forms: white with purple-red or carmine blotches; white with veins so close as to give the illusion of grey, and pure white. Hildebrand (1898) referred to flowers changing colour from pink to white or vice versa between one season and the next. However, according to my own observations, only plants carrying heterozygous genes for flower colour produce blooms which change from white to pink. Homozygous whites do not change. Further experiments would be useful.

Fertilisation and the Fruit

The male and female parts of the flower can easily be seen with the naked eye. The single, central stigma extends from a superior ovary which contains many ovules. There is free basal placentation and no division of ovary. The male part of the flower consists of five stamens which are situated close to the ovary. The large anthers which can be yellow, brown or purple in appearance, according to species, are pressed close to the style and when mature, dust-like pollen drifts to the top of the sticky stigma in the slightest breeze or knock of the flower. Insects also assist in cross-pollination. They are drawn to the flowers by the bright colour of the corolla or the strong fragrance, and carry the pollen on their legs and bodies from one flower to another. Once the pollen reaches the stigma, the male cells fertilise the female cells or ovules in the ovary at the foot of the style. A phenomenon known as parthenogenesis is also thought to occur (see Glossary).

Fertilised ovules develop into seeds inside a fruit which is botanically called a capsule rather than a seed-pod. Each capsule matures to the size of a pea: large, in the case of *graecum* and *persicum*; average, in *hederifolium*, *africanum* and *commutatum*; and small, in other species.

The development of the capsules takes many weeks or months: first the corolla drops to the ground, then the flower stem starts to coil, sometimes trapping a leaf or another flower as it curls. Apart from three exceptions, the coiling commences at the flower head end of the stem, taking the immature capsule down to soil level and often right into the grit in which the parent plant is growing. Two of the exceptions are *graecum* and *rohlfsianum*, which begin to coil at the tuber end of the stem, drawing the capsule downwards, often leaving part of the flower stalk or pedicel uncoiled with the result that the capsule is stretched out a short way from the parent plant — perhaps an extra aid in seed dispersal. In *persicum*, the third exception, the capsule is deposited even further from the parent, since the flower stem doesn't coil at all. It stiffens and then bends slowly down to the ground, so that the seeds are placed at a distance from the tuber.

In nature, the capsule splits when it is ripe; but the brown seeds are also removed by ants and other insects, attracted to the sticky jelly-like substance which surrounds them. Birds also act as seed dispersal agents, when removing moss from around the plants.

Seeds germinate surprisingly well if the outer coverings of the capsule simply rot away in damp summer weather. Another method of dispersal occurs when the tight coils suddenly slacken just before the capsule ripens, allowing a slight spring action, thus sending the seeds a short distance away. However, this can only happen when the capsule has not been buried in the coiling down process weeks or months earlier. Detailed study of ripening capsules seems to suggest that the coiling of pedicels after flowering is more to protect the developing seeds than to aid dispersal. The capsules are drawn back under foliage out of the sight of birds.

CHAPTER 2

Cultivation

The well-known gardener and bulb-grower E.A. Bowles was referring to *Cyclamen hederifolium* when he wrote in 1949 for the Royal Horticultural Society's Journal: 'it pays rent for eleven months out of the twelve.' This is often quoted and misquoted, so what a pity he wasn't able to make a similar comment on the genus as a whole! Now, however, it is possible to have cyclamen in flower during every season. And when we think of the evergreen *purpurascens* and the fascinating variety of foliage found in all the species, it can be seen that cyclamen pay rent for *twelve* months of the year. But we have learnt more about cyclamen than was known in Bowles' day.

What is the best way to begin growing cyclamen? This is not an easy question, as there is more than one right way to start. You might strike lucky and have immediate success from a handful of dry tubers, as I did, but it is usually considered safer to start with growing plants.

Although I have been a gardener since I was eight years old, when my mathematician father used to walk round a walled garden before breakfast talking algebra to his plants, my interest in alpines — and cyclamen in particular — came much later. My first cyclamen were obtained and planted without ceremony. I found some little shrivelled tubers in Woolworths and dug them into the open garden with minimum fuss. To my surprise, several delicate flowers on fragile-looking stems emerged months later when I had forgotten about purchasing the tubers. I was completely captivated by the brave show in rather rough surroundings; but the memory of this experience was to lie dormant in my mind until I met Dr A.K. Wells some years later. He introduced me to the cyclamen and other alpines which he had collected since his retirement from King's College, London, where he lectured on geology for many years. His wonderful way of teaching by example led to my own development of a deeper interest in these plants.

But I was to learn later that my experience with the Woolworths' tubers was only beginner's luck. Sometimes dry tubers can be quite difficult to bring back into growth. At the Cyclamen Society Conference in 1978, it was reported that a tuber of *graecum* had remained alive with no leaf or flower for six years and a specimen of *cilicium* had produced new signs of growth after four years.

Before considering how to buy, plant and grow cyclamen, let us turn our attention to the basic requirements in the way of equipment.

Equipment

A collection of containers will be required by the gardener who raises an assortment of species and varieties from seed. Clay pots and pans are the most pleasing for mature specimens of the species, and they are available in a wide range of size, shape and ornamentation. Pans are comparatively simple in shape and most useful for seedlings, slow-growing or shallow-rooting forms of cyclamen. Plain clay pots and pans are preferred on the show bench. Plastic pots are generally favoured by the growers of the cultivated strains of *persicum*. Again, numerous types of pot are available, from the very plain to highly ornamental. Colour is a point to watch with plastic, since brightly coloured pots tend to detract from the delicate shades of the flowers.

Various modern items have been found serviceable for raising quantities of seedlings. The Plantpak Modular System is both economical and labour-saving, as well as being hygienic and convenient. Large seeds may be sown straight into the small size expanded polystyrene units, or potted on into the larger sizes. Many units fit neatly into one well-drained tray, and several trays will go neatly into either a cold frame or glasshouse.

The Jiffy range of products is also recommended. The compressed pellets look like thick flat coins until they are watered, then they swell into little pot-shaped blocks of peat. The correct amounts of fertiliser for healthy plant growth have already been added, and seedlings can be left until the roots start to emerge through the net that contains the peat. There is only one danger: the speed at which the pots dry out. Correct watering is important, especially with cyclamen. When the colour of the peat begins to go pale, more water should be added. Seedlings may be potted on without removing them from the net; this ensures that the roots suffer no disturbance.

Plant labels are a necessary extra. Carefully recorded names and dates of sowing or transplanting will add to the ease and pleasure of gardening. An indelible marker should preferably be used.

A cold frame is the most useful piece of gardening equipment for growing the hardy species, and indeed some of the more tender species can thrive if protected from excess rain by a cold frame. There are various sizes and shapes of readymade frames available on

31

the market. The majority are manufactured from extruded aluminium sections glazed either with glass or with outdoor horticultural clear acrylic sheets.

Figure 2.1
A Typical Cold
Frame

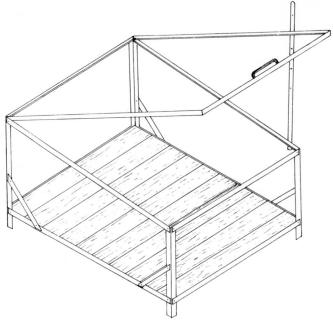

The do-it-yourself enthusiast might decide to construct a cold frame to suit his/her own requirements. The frame shown in Figure 2.1 is made from aluminium sections and glazed with clear acrylic sheets. It has the special feature of a raised wooden floor: this gives some warmth and also prevents slugs and snails from getting into the frame and devouring the plants. The floor is removable.

Aluminium is a light metal with excellent durability and strength. It is available in various sizes of section, is easy to work with, hygienic, non-toxic, non-absorbent and does not rot or rust. It also needs no painting! Outdoor horticultural clear acrylic sheets are available in thicknesses of 2.5 mm and 4 mm. It is also easy to cut, shape and fit. If you decide to build your own frame, it is financially more beneficial to buy complete lengths of aluminium section and full size sheets and cut them to your own requirements at home.

Having decided on the size of the frame, draw an isometric diagram showing all the necessary dimensions. For the construction of a frame about 1 m square in area and approximately 0.5 m high, use aluminium sections about 25 mm across. Cut the sections to the lengths required, and file all sharp edges and drill one hole per connection. Assemble the frame using countersunk stainless screws and nuts. Next, measure for sheet size, then cut and fit sheets using glazing clips or self-tapping screws — in which case the sheets would have to be pre-drilled: two screws each side of the sheet will be sufficient. For a hinged lid, fit a handle, including a stay, to keep the lid open. Place the timber floor boards on the bearer without fixing.

A greenhouse is almost essential if a quantity of the cultivated strains of *Cyclamen persicum* are to be grown satisfactorily. But where there is no garden, a few pots may be kept continuously on a light windowsill, or a number of plants can be successfully raised in a conservatory or glass home extension. Choose a glass-to-ground type of structure for maximum shelf space in the light: aluminium has the advantage of being easy to maintain. Staging, to stand pots on, and capillary matting, to aid watering, should also be considered carefully before purchase.

Many local nurseries or garden centres will not be able to supply all species of cyclamen, and the best way to start is to buy growing plants from a specialist nursery, which will be able to provide a wider choice. A list of such nurseries is given in Useful Addresses (page 134). Most nurseries charge for their catalogues nowadays, to cover printing and postage costs. But the lists of rare plants and bulbs — sometimes with useful notes — are so delightful that they are well worth the cost involved.

How to Buy

As far as cyclamen is concerned, the words 'growing plants' can mean one of three things — all acceptable. You might open a neat little parcel to find perfect plants in full bloom looking as if they had never been disturbed from the pots or open ground where they were growing before packing. Or you might receive a well-padded Jiffy bag containing tubers — leaves and roots attached — mixed with damp peat and pearlite in polythene bags, labelled according to species. The third possibility is a flat package containing freshly lifted tubers with roots but no top growth. All should grow away satisfactorily, providing the cyclamen are removed from the bags and potted up or planted out soon after arrival.

Starting with Seeds

Cyclamen can be grown easily from seed; however, the problem for the beginner is to obtain the seed when it is just ripe. Germination occurs much more freely when the seed is sown while it is still sticky and recently plucked from the capsule, rather than when it has been kept dry for some time. Another difficulty is that little seed is readily available — especially of the less common forms. Unless you have a gardening friend anxious to give you a supply of rare seed, probably the only way you could be sure of acquiring fresh seed would be by joining the Cyclamen Society. The larger seed firms sell

Cultivation

seed of the popular cyclamen species. This has been found to germinate if a little preparation is given to the bought seed before sowing (see Propagation).

The size of cyclamen seed varies, according to the species, from the tiny pin-head specks of *repandum* to the comparatively large seeds of *graecum*, which are about 2 mm across. The seed of *balearicum* is a little larger than *repandum*. It is quite easy to handle the seeds in order to separate them for sowing in pots or pans. It is also possible for the more expert gardener to know what he is likely to have been given by glancing at the seed in a packet; there is an obvious difference in size between the smallest seed and the largest. But it would be more difficult to tell *hederifolium* from *coum* simply by looking at the seed. In most cases, it is necessary to accept whatever is given in good faith. A few surprises will occur, no doubt, but they should be taken as part of the excitement of raising any plant from seed.

When to Buy

Cyclamen plants may be purchased at any time. However, some specialists state in their catalogues that tubers will only be lifted during the period May to November. This is because the ground is too hard to work during the winter, but pot-grown specimens can be safely bought at any time of year. In both cases, it is sensible to order well in advance, as many of the rarer species sell out quickly.

Although seed may be sown during any month, especially if propagators are used for the tender species, rapid germination is more likely to occur when sowing takes place during summer or early autumn; therefore, seed of the species should be ordered in spring or early summer. Seed of some miniature cultivated strains of *persicum* can be sown in February or March for flowers nine months later; but seed of the giant-flowering strains is usually sown in August. Hybrids are now sown at regular intervals throughout the year for flowers during all seasons.

Dry tubers will be obtained most easily during mid-summer as this is the season when cyclamen rest naturally, although it has been noted that at least one nurseryman only lists cyclamen in his spring catalogue.

Mixing the Compost

One aspect of gardening is too often taken for granted and skimped. Success or failure depends to a large extent on careful attention to soil requirements of individual plants. In their natural habitat, cyclamen are found on a variety of soil types, on limestone rock and in screes and leaf moulds of various kinds. Although cyclamen will thrive in slightly acid or alkaline soils, they do seem to do better

34

and become established more quickly in a balanced compost. Free drainage is also important.

A good general compost for the hardy species can be made up at home. The all-purpose cyclamen compost that Mrs D.E. Saunders recommends in the Alpine Garden Society Guide is a little too open with the result that young plants dry out rather more quickly than they should. It is difficult to get the mixture just right, i.e. neither too colloidal or sticky, nor too porous and open. The following compost has been found satisfactory:

One part leaf mould
One part fibrous peat
One part horticultural sand, i.e. not builder's sand or sea-sand
One part limestone grit
One part John Innes Compost

This mixture feels light and airy when you run it through your fingers. When well made, it looks good and smells good. John Innes compost that has been used once for growing summer annuals in pots can be chosen in place of newly purchased or mixed soil. It is widely recognised that the tender house plant cyclamen are heavy feeders, yet many gardeners refuse to accept that hardy cyclamen also do better when given some well-rotted manure. However, my own experience shows that although it is not necessary to mix manure in the potting compost a top-dressing of bone-meal or composted cow manure is beneficial. Dare I say that rabbit manure also works wonders? (Rabbits are considered such a pest by many gardeners, that the droppings they leave behind are not valued as beneficial. In any case, they do not seem to enjoy eating cyclamen.) Either way, cyclamen respond more to a regular annual top dressing than a rich compost underneath the tuber. This is partly due to the fact that the roots on many species are at the top and sides of the tuber.

The cultivated hybrid strains of *persicum* may also be planted in the compost recommended for the hardy species. However, the large-flowered strains are usually given a compost which contains considerably more humus. Here is a suitable mixture:

Two parts loam or home-made compost
One part leaf mould
One part horticultural sand
One part finely broken clay pots
One part well-rotted farmyard or rabbit manure

Cultivation

Add the equivalent of one dessert-spoonful of ground chalk to every bucketful of the mixture and turn over thoroughly with a spade.

It can be seen that large greenhouse plants require a fair quantity of fertiliser or manure to produce those gigantic blooms that are so popular during the dark months of the year. Alternatively, the small-flowered strains can be grown successfully in light soil-less composts. However, it should be realised that, in this case, gardeners give regular feeds of liquid fertiliser from an early stage in the development of the plants.

Some nurserymen advocate moving cyclamen seedlings on into John Innes Potting Compost. This can be purchased ready-mixed, or can be made up at home as follows:

7 buckets of loam
3 buckets of leaf mould or peat
2 buckets of sand

The size of bucket is not important, as it is the proportions rather than the weight that matters. Mix well before adding 112 gm John Innes Base per 36 litres. Four 9 litre buckets will hold this amount.

Drainage

All cyclamen require adequate drainage. Plenty of grit or fibrous substance is essential in any soil used for cyclamen. No matter how good the compost or the plants, unless the water is able to run away freely from around the tuber, heavy plant loss will result. If the soil around cyclamen is sticky with clay, or the hole in the base of the pot is blocked, the tuber will almost certainly rot. It is well worth taking pains to master the art of good drainage. Once this basic requirement is satisfied, most cyclamen thrive and grow for years — possibly a lifetime — without further trouble.

In the garden, if the land is not naturally well-drained, it might be advisable to dig out the proposed area and incorporate loose stones, rock chippings or rubble in the subsoil; although this rather drastic treatment will only be thought worthwhile in limited spaces, such as terrace borders, etc. In small gardens, a comparatively new idea is to make raised beds or low, open-topped double walls, where a considerable amount of drainage material is used between the foundations.

One test for adequate drainage that can easily be applied to cyclamen plants in pots is to watch carefully and notice how long the water remains on top of the soil. If it lingers in little pools on the surface — even for a minute or so — there is not enough grit or other drainage material in the compost. Water should disappear into the soil almost as fast as it is poured on to the top of the pot. It is usually loam or clay that causes waterlogged conditions.

It cannot be stressed too strongly that irrespective of soil, situation or climate, cyclamen thrive best if given sufficient drainage material below and around the tubers and roots.

Growing cyclamen in cool climates means that many species will have to be kept continuously in containers, and will flourish so long as the soil is well-drained. As mentioned earlier, clay pots and pans, rather than plastic, do seem to suit the hardy species, especially those that are grown without cover on the terrace. The cultivated strains of *persicum* have been raised equally well in either type of container, and most of the nursery plants are grown in plastic pots nowadays.

Size of pot is more important than might be realised by the beginner. For example, cyclamen seedlings will grow more successfully when one large pan is used rather than lots of little pots. Several seedlings to one pot or pan are less likely to be lost than a solitary seedling in one pot, because, as so much drainage is necessary, a small amount of compost is liable to dry out too quickly.

Potting Up and Repotting

Figure 2.2
C. graecum

Turning to mature tubers, a deep pot — once known as a Long Tom — will be necessary for *graecum*, as this species has a long tap root. *C. purpurascens* and *repandum* will need taller and larger pots than say *hederifolium* or *coum*, and should be planted 15 cm and 5 cm deep respectively. For the other species, the smaller tubers should be planted in 7.5 cm pots and the larger tubers in 10, 12.5, 15 or 30 cm pots. Always bear in mind that cyclamen tend to flower more prolifically when they are slightly potbound; they should not be grown in very large containers in comparison to the size of tuber.

When planting, first make sure that the pot is well scrubbed, with no sign of green-mould or calcium deposit. Only containers with drainage holes should be used for cyclamen, and a small square of perforated zinc should be placed over the drainage hole (this is to keep out the worms and woodlice). Cover the zinc with a good handful of chippings, choosing limestone for preference. Then trowel in a layer of the light soil and grit mixture described above. Shake well down and plant the tuber – rounded, smooth side *down*. Only just cover with soil and finish with a generous layer of chippings. Finally, give the pot a good watering and be sure to label as you work. There is nothing more frustrating than trying to recall *what* you planted *where* a few months or even weeks later!

Cyclamen do best if they are not moved too often. It is true that you can dig up a plant from the garden when it is flowering, pack it into a pot and take it to a show, or place it on a living room windowsill, without causing the specimen to die. However, you might find that a plant so treated will not perform properly the following year. Perhaps the leaves will be few in number, or small, and the flowers non-existent. It is better to grow some plants especially for showing or display in the house and greenhouse. And try to leave the potting-on of seedlings, or the repotting of established plants, until the tuber has really outgrown a small container.

Choose a fine – but not too hot – day in the first half of summer for moving the early autumn and winter-flowering species; at this time of year, the tubers will be resting and the least damage will be done to the roots and delicate shoots. However, one autumn-flowering species – *rohlfsianum* – is best left undisturbed during early summer: it has been found it flowers more freely if it is not moved from old compost into new until frequent and regular watering begins again in late summer, for the start of a fresh flowering season. It is best to move the spring-flowering species during October and the evergreen summer-flowering *purpurascens* seems to respond to a spring move, just when the worst of the winter weather is over and the early sunshine is beginning to warm the soil. Make sure that you repot this species before the middle of May. In every case, always try to repot plants before they begin their flowering season – before the little buds begin to hook up – remembering that new growth commences weeks ahead of the time the plants are in full bloom.

The delights of watching the day-to-day development of plants in the garden are best learnt by experience. Cyclamen remain with you for a lifetime, improving with each year that passes. Every season more flowers appear and more self-sown seedlings begin to bloom, until the garden contains a carpet of fragile petals in the most delicate colours. And a number of different species coming into flower month after month means that there is always a new bud about to open. The coldest days will not prevent the hardiest species from producing perfect buds in winter. This year, *C. coum* delighted us by unfolding just as soon as the snow melted. The flowers were undamaged by frost. Other hardy species flowered on the kitchen windowsill, their fragrance drifting down to me as I washed the dishes; and in the greenhouse and bulb frame the flowers of the wild species were everywhere brightening the scene. Indoors beautiful, delicate cyclamen were to be seen in every direction: pale, miniature, frilled, clear-coloured and fragrant petals.

But the fact that cyclamen are winter- and spring-flowering plants is well known, whereas perhaps it is not so widely realised that there is enjoyment to be gained from growing plants of this genus during all the seasons of the year. What interest will they give me in the summer, you might wonder. Here is a record of cyclamen in the garden from June to September — the diary shows the gradual development of seedlings and resting plants as they begin to come into bloom.

14 June. The first cyclamen flower opened on *fatrense* today. There are many flower buds to follow and some leaves have remained on the plants since last year; new leaves began to appear as soon as the frosts finished, which was early as usual.

21 June. The *purpurascens* buds are developing more quickly as we reach mid-summer. Some plants have been truly evergreen — many leaves persisting through the coldest months, although they have been completely unprotected outside — others have lost all but one or two leaves. One plant has a seed capsule and a single leaf. It doesn't seem to make any difference whether the leaves of this species are plain or patterned as far as evergreen qualities are concerned, some of each keep their leaves through spring and summer. (It is worth mentioning here that early summer is the time when most of the other species lose their leaves. It is certainly useful to have *purpurascens* foliage as ground cover in the garden during summer.)

One plant of *persicum* has also been evergreen this year, which is most unusual, especially as it is the florists' kind.

Cultivation

28 June. Cyclamen hederifolium have started to bud up. Tiny little swollen blobs can be seen emerging from large tubers where the topsoil has been blown adrift. Some of the tubers were so large that they have spread right across to the rims of their pots. These needed repotting into one-size wider pots. When lifted, new white roots could be observed just pushing out from the sides of the tubers. It was pleasing to realise that the job had been done at a time when the plants would benefit most from fresh compost.

A seed-tray of first-year and second-year *parviflorum* was covered with dark peaty soil. The small tubers were still healthy — a great relief! — although without leaves. Birds uncovered them while pulling out moss for their nests in the early spring. Half of the plants were uprooted and scattered during the bird-raid; but most had been retrieved soon afterwards and replanted.

A tray of *cilicium* first-year seedlings needed top-dressing with grit. These have also lost their leaves, but the tubers seem hard.

The flower buds of *purpurascens* are showing their colour, but they are not ready to unfold yet. *C. fatrense* are in full bloom with the young leaves developing nicely. They might be a suitable entry for the summer horticultural show in the village.

5 July. The buds of *purpurascens* are developing rapidly; they are almost at the point of opening. The first flowers of the season on *fatrense* have already dropped. Minute buds can be seen on the tops of *intaminatum* tubers and *hederifolium* are showing further signs of growth.

Capsules on the Wye College mini-cyclamen of the *persicum* species have ripened and the seeds are in soak ready for sowing. Large capsules on giant strains of *persicum* have split and the glistening brown seeds are ripe and ready to drop.

It was interesting to note that the capsules on one *hederifolium* plant were twice the size of the capsules on another plant of the same species, but of a different colour. The *album* had the largest capsules and the pink the smallest; but it could easily be the other way around, since the white is a form not a cultivar and therefore variable, i.e. you can find large whites and small whites. Both of these plants have been pot-grown; both have the same compost, and both pots are in the same shady part of the garden.

12 July. Arrival of the Cyclamen Society's Journal with a seed exchange form enclosed drew my attention to the number of ripening capsules on the hardy species. Most seem to be making new top-growth. When the stone chippings were tipped off *coum*, the new, thin shoots could be seen lying flat against the tuber, but not yet reaching for the light. It is important to appreciate that the winter-flowering species begin to grow in the middle of summer.

Flower buds are developing on *africanum*, *cilicium*, *hederifolium*, *intaminatum* and *mirabile*. The leaves have gone from the *repandum* yearling seedlings and from the *graecum* mature plants. The latter must get a good baking on the tops of the tubers. The pots are standing in trays of moist gravel and water is being given only via the base, i.e. not over the top of the tuber. It is also time to stand the *rohlfsianum* pot in shallow water to encourage new growth.

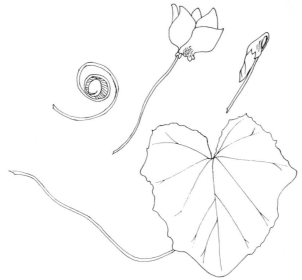

Figure 2.3
C. africanum

C. purpurascens are in full flower. New leaves are appearing daily, but the plants are hanging on to their yellowing foliage of last season. However, *fatrense* have fresh green leaves, the old leaves shrivelled rather than dropped: the plants seem reluctant to part with them. The first capsules have already coiled down, though they will not ripen for a whole year. It is amazing to observe the baby capsules of this season just beginning to develop beside the swollen, ripe capsules of the flower crop of the previous year.

14 July. A white *hederifolium* in flower — perhaps the earliest of the species recorded this year. (No: a letter from the editor of the Cyclamen Society's Journal reports an earlier one in his garden.)

15 July. Today, realised that the number of capsules a plant is carrying seems not to affect the earliness or lateness of flowering, as once was thought: some tubers bearing capsules have no new season's top growth at all yet, while others with the same number of capsules have numerous flower buds well up.

It is encouraging to see the strong pink pedicels on so many cyclamen already poking up through the stone chippings. They indicate that it will be a good year for autumn-flowering species.

Careful examination reveals marked differences in the colour of young tubers. Second-year *cilicium* appear light brown, a hazel shade, and the little roots have begun to grow, although there are no new leaves yet and no flower buds on the babies — mature plants of this species have tiny buds beginning to emerge. Second-year *hederifolium* are larger than the *cilicium* (most are twice the size and all have been grown outside with no cover) and they are chestnut brown at this stage. But it is the second-year *parviflorum* that are the most spectacular: they are a bright, almost transparent, bead-like green. This was quite a surprise — they are so different from other cyclamen.

A few seeds of the tender Wye College miniatures and an equally small number of other selected strains of *persicum* were sown early as an experiment.

10 August. Returned from abroad today. The garden has been well cared for in the meantime, but dramatic changes have taken place in the cyclamen. Violent contrasts of weather must have affected the speed of growth. There have been days of warm weather, then wet, then warm again, followed by a day of heat wave and a day of torrential rain, merging into days of continuous rain.

More cyclamen flowers have opened, although it is still too early for most forms of the autumn-flowering species under shrubs to be in bloom. Moving from pot to pot to observe the beauty and any development in growth, damage from pests or losses from the resting season, there was something to attract my attention on every plant.

In the greenhouse, *cyprium* which showed no sign of life above the stone chippings in July are now producing their buds. Moisture in the gravel around *graecum* has been maintained in my absence, and the tubers have received the necessary baking from the sun during the heat wave, while the fleshy roots remained in contact with water; new top growth has begun to appear.

Pests among greenhouse pots, such as snails, were easily picked off by hand; but it is a problem deciding what to do with the poor creatures! Luckily, little damage has been done, in fact they seem to have cleared the greenmould from the side of a pot, but moss and liverwort will have to be removed from some of the containers again. Seed-trays are disappointing: the Wye College seed sown before departure has not germinated yet, although hopefully it will in time.

Pots in the bulb frame and on paving are flourishing — plants are fully in flower where only tiny cyclamen buds had been present in mid-July, apart from the summer-flowering species and an unusually early form of *hederifolium*. Now there are more *hederifolium* and these have been joined by *cilicium* var. *intaminatum*. The *purpurascens* are all out and the flowers of *fatrense* have curled down their heads. The capsules look healthy, although at this early date, they are only half the size that they should reach at maturity next spring. The seeds of last year's capsules on *hederifolium* and *purpurascens* have dehisced over the parent plants; some are flowering through a carpet of seeds; others are just showing buds through a mass of sticky seed that has scattered unevenly over the soil.

The most pleasing sight was a pot of the rarest form of *coum* var. *caucasicum*. This plant had lost all its leaves during a frosty spell at the beginning of the year and, as the tuber was small, survival seemed unlikely. What delight to discover this precious cyclamen is still alive!

The almost as rare *coum* 371 has one leaf fully extended, displaying the lovely wide silver margin characteristic of the form. However, unfortunately, large bite-marks mar the magnificence of the pattern. A quick check among nearby pots soon revealed the culprit: a large round-shelled snail was found sleeping the light hours away. Other more common forms of *coum* are surprisingly advanced in leaf; but, as expected, *balearicum*, *creticum*, *libanoticum*, *pseudibericum* and *repandum* show no sign of renewed growth, since they flower later in the spring.

The almost unobtainable *parviflorum* have come through the summer. They have not been allowed to dry out and the roots are still alive and active. Tubers in their third year appear to be carrying minute flower buds. This will be something to watch with great excitement; but further confirmation at a later date is necessary, as it is rather optimistic to expect flowers on three-year-old plants and they are so small. However, the number of seedlings that have survived winter cold and summer heat is encouraging. Since the seeds were sown, the trays have been on paving against a north-east facing wall, which receives only the minimum of early morning sun. The compost is peaty and inclined to become covered with moss. The tubers have been exposed to the elements because a bird picked off the moss for her nest in the spring, so that they were dry at the top and buried in moist soil at the base. When the trays were lifted an assortment of pests stirred on the lower side: two different types of slugs, a flat-shelled snail and several woodlice. All were hurriedly removed.

Trays of third-year *hederifolium* are just beginning to shoot; *cilicium* seedlings are slow starting, although their close relatives *intaminatum* have already put up, still tiny, second-year leaves — the plain forms slightly in advance of the patterned-leaf forms. Ordinary *coum* second-year seedlings are also showing tiny leaves and both cultivated strains and species forms of *persicum* are beginning to grow more quickly again after a semi-resting period, when they have received natural rainfall. None were dried off. At first glance, plants in the shade seemed more leafy than plants in half-sun; but when the leaves of the specimens in the shade were moved, the foliage fell off, leaving the tubers without buds of any kind. No doubt these would produce flowers, but they would be late next spring, while the plants that have received some sunlight already have new season's leaves and flower buds well started; they will probably be in bloom by late autumn and continue to flower through the winter.

13 August. A silvery track and further damage to leaves indicated that another large snail or slug was living undetected among the outdoor collection of pots. A complete clean-up of the area was necessary to find the intruder. Snails have been more troublesome than usual this summer. There have been very few in previous years. At least they are easy to remove, but if many more appear the RSPB slug killer containers will have to be used. These attract slugs with beer or cider. Half a grapefruit placed hollow side down also traps them, but they are unsightly. Slug pellets are the last resort, on account of the birds; even if the pellets are hidden under pots, and the dead removed daily and put in the dustbin, there might be a slight risk that one would crawl to a position where a bird could peck it up and die from the poison. Natural control methods are used as far as possible. Someone suggested a hedgehog and this idea greatly appeals. They do come sometimes, then after a few days they wander off seeming to prefer a nomadic life.

Many birds come to the garden: blackbirds, blue tits, cole tits, doves, thrushes, one green finch, one jay, magpies, pigeons, robins, sparrows, starlings and one wren. (When we looked at them against the snow the following winter, we were surprised to see that some of the blue tits were ringed. The RSPB is recording their movements.)

14 August. Tracked down the last slug — a huge specimen — and swept the paving after washing the dirt and moss off all the pots.

Sowed more *persicum* and tried to salvage some of the self-sown scattered seeds from the tops of parents plants of the hardy species for the Cyclamen Society seed exchange.

Checked that compost in the greenhouse pots is sufficiently moist on this very hot day — much too hot for cyclamen flowers under glass. The flowers outside look cool and fresh. Most of the autumn-flowering hardy species are moving rapidly into full flower in the shade.

27 August. A visit to Wye College resulted in a happy afternoon looking at a carefully kept cyclamen collection. The weather was warm and the sun shone quite strongly through a hazy mist. The effect of the slight difference in climate between Essex and Kent was clear: the cyclamen at Wye were a few weeks advanced in development.

Walking through the long glasshouse, cyclamen could be seen arranged on benches, covered with capillary matting, down both sides of a central path. My attention was drawn to the giant *africanum* tubers which were growing in the largest size pans. One was in a rather shallow container until a suitable 30 cm clay pot could be found. Several had flowers already in bloom and there were many buds and leaves to come in the months ahead.

Various foliage patterns on *graecum* were pointed out and a leaf almost without markings stood out for its plainness. The rich, velvety texture on other leaves was just beginning to develop, although the buds and leaves of the new season were still quite young with only a few open on each plant. The base of the pots had been kept moist through the summer.

Moving next to *coum*, it was interesting to note that the foliage was already well up and spread out over the pebble topping on the pots, yet this winter-flowering species did not appear to be wilting in the heat of summer under glass.

Cyclamen hederifolium were grouped according to flower colour, *album* coming before the *roseum*. Lots of white flowers with less pink: this was partly because the white were flowering before the pink. The white was pure without the hint of carmine that can sometimes exist around the sinus of the *album*, although there was one plant with a white corolla and a deep carmine 'nose'. However, this was thought to be due to the bleaching of the petals from pale pink by the strong sunlight. Many pink blooms lose their colour this way: a point to remember where glasshouse cultivation of cyclamen is concerned.

There was a row of seedlings of the variety 'Bowles' Apollo', although it was not possible to see the pattern, as it was still early for *hederifolium* foliage to be unfolding. There were also scented forms and the flowers were very fragrant. Next came rows and rows of seedlings at first-, second- and third-year stages. Plants sown at the beginning of year one were producing a few blooms at the end of year two, and flowering well in the autumn of the third year — much earlier results than usually considered possible. Liquid fertiliser was used regularly.

An unexpected delight was a fine specimen of *rohlfsianum* with four flower buds, which were eagerly counted and praised in appreciation of the rarity and splendour of the species.

Cultivation

Small groups of *balearicum*, *creticum*, *cyprium*, *mirabile* and *repandum* were passed without comment, as growth was either non-existent or just commencing. The fragrance of *purpurascens* was exceptionally strong, probably due to the sunshine and the fact that several plants were covered with ruby-coloured flowers. The form *fatrense* with lots of plain green leaves and large flowers looked healthy.

A rare form of *coum* with entirely silver foliage had been placed separately from the common forms, as it was being tested to see if it would breed true.

28 August. While pulling moss from the top of a pot of *cilicium* var. *intaminatum* some seeds were found between the green of the weed and the dark damp soil underneath. One of the capsules must have dehisced unobserved and the seeds scattered before the moss grew up and covered the harvest. Great effort was made to find every seed, since this is the rarer variegated form with rather well-marked leaves. When some of the moss fell on the grass below, a frantic search through the turf for a lost seed was like looking for a needle in a haystack. A glistening brown shape was spotted, but not retrieved as it slipped through the grass roots into a crack in the earth. But eventually ten other seeds were removed from around the tuber of the parent by a method of washing teaspoons of soil in a shallow dish of water, rather like panning for gold! It was easier to detect the bright colour of the clean seed.

29 August. Removed the moss and liverwort from a pan in the greenhouse containing *cilicium* P.D. 25889. The plant was grown from a packet of seed distributed in the first Cyclamen Society seed exchange. The Peloponnese form of *repandum* had been sown to one side of the pan in 1978, but whereas the *cilicium* germinated the same autumn within weeks of sowing, *repandum* cotyledons did not emerge until over a year later, and further seedlings appeared two years after sowing. The *cilicium* flowered for the first time in autumn 1980. Now, in their second flowering season, there are flower buds in profusion: some almost in bloom; some no more than tiny pedicels with dot-like knobs for buds. How exciting it is when flower buds are found on cyclamen which have been grown from seed.

The *C. repandum* var. *rhodense* is beginning to show top growth. It is so very rare in cultivation that it lives a solitary existence on a cool windowsill indoors, growing and flowering well. Perhaps it would set seed out of doors, but as plants of this form are scarce, it is a risk to put them outside in case of an unexpectedly severe frost. The plant will be among the most interesting to watch in the house during the coming months.

46

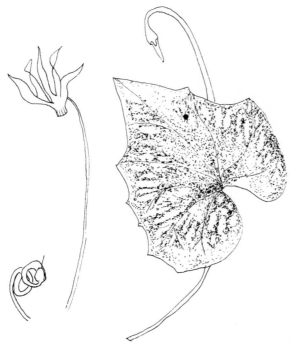

Figure 2.4
C. repandum var.
rhodense

(The Wye College mini-cyclamen *persicum* sown in July did ger-minate — in an unheated greenhouse at the beginning of November! This was unusually slow, possibly the temperature was too high during the summer, since high temperatures inhibit germination. At 62°-65°F Wye College hybrids germinate within four to six weeks. Hardy cyclamen seed sown in trays in July and September also germinated in the first week of November, and other seedlings were found around the garden: some had obviously been dispersed by ants and birds. People who had bought my plants, or rooted cuttings of shrubs, from the stall of the local horticultural society, reported finding cyclamen seedlings in the pots a few weeks later as an extra bonus.)

Care of the Flowering Plant Throughout the Year

Flowers appear year after year on cyclamen once the plants are well established. A plant that is flowering for the first time will put up two or three flowers, and each year after the number should increase until fifty or more rise triumphantly from one tuber. Cyclamen flowers are undoubtedly fragile yet they unfold their delicate petals in mid-winter frost or mid-summer heat. They flourish with little or no attention once established; but if extra care is given the freshness of the colour and the fragrance of each individual bloom will last longer.

Cultivation

In the Spring

The flowers will still be in full bloom on *persicum*. Watch for late frosts and attend to moulds immediately, since cold and damp can easily lead to spotting on the corollas which spoils the look of otherwise fine plants.

Sudden spells of early morning strong sunshine can cause the petals to fade and lose their main attraction. A strain noted for its deep-pink or violet blooms will not be the same if it becomes a wishy-washy pink or unappealing washed-out magenta. The greenhouse should be shaded if the temperature is likely to rise above 70°F and heated if expected to fall below 40°F. Otherwise, plants do best in full light at this time of year. Give them regular doses of liquid fertiliser as long as there are flower buds still growing.

Species *persicum* rather than the cultivated strains will flower out of doors during March or April, and even into May in cool countries, providing a sheltered place is chosen on well-drained ground. In England, flowering outside has been recorded in the southern half of the country. The main danger is likely to be frost, as the tubers are not hardy; but slugs are another hazard. Some gardeners find that their plants produce leaves and flower buds in dry stone walls and on rockeries, but that the first severe frost of the year weakens the tissue of both the petioles and corollas so that they collapse. In warm countries, this species is sometimes grown in shade houses made from bamboo leaves and brushwood, or neat structures of slatted wood. In New Zealand, where the climate is similar to Britain, shade houses are used to give some protection against frost as well as sun. It is worth noting that in Africa shade houses are used to shelter pot plants from the sun, but wild *persicum* grows without protection other than the natural screen provided by shrubs and trees.

Houseplant *persicum*, including the miniature strains and the giant-flowering cultivars, will continue to bloom cheerfully into early summer if kept on a light windowsill in a cool room. Problems which might arise include attacks of *botrytis* (see Chapter 7) and lengthening of petioles due to the lack of light. One answer to this difficulty is to form the habit of giving the pots half a turn every day, as you check to see if water is required. This way all the foliage receives a maximum share of available light.

Besides *persicum* in the alpine house or greenhouse, there will be the tender species *balearicum*, *creticum* and *libanoticum* in full flower. Species *pseudibericum* and *repandum* might also be in the sheltered warmth of a glasshouse, although they flower away merrily in the open, even in a cool climate.

One of the rarest delights is to open an alpine house door in early spring and be met with the delicious fragrance of *libanoticum*, or *repandum rhodense*, and the rich red-pink of *pseudibericum* flowers. In a mixed greenhouse, the latter looks lovely with miniature narcissus, silver saxifrage *grisebachii* and early flowering auriculas and primulas. Greenhouse windows should be open at all times except when frost is on the ground or expected overnight. In an unheated glasshouse, newspapers are an economical way of saving flowers and plants. Arrange the pots so that they are close together in a group. Then place four large pots so that they become corner supports for a temporary structure made of wire-netting or string netting pinned on to a wooden square frame. Several thicknesses of newspaper of good quality can then be laid on top of the frame to give extra protection from the weather during short frosty periods. However, this should be removed at every opportunity to allow adequate air and light to reach the plants.

Hot, burning sunlight is equally damaging as frost to half-hardy species of cyclamen, especially to the thin leaves of *balearicum*. Counteract this by arranging some form of shade if the glasshouse is situated in a part of the garden where it catches the full sun every day, as so many of them are. *C. repandum* is another species that is likely to shrivel in scorching sun.

Spring-flowering species in cold frames will benefit from having the lights lifted during warm, sunny days; newspaper will be needed over the plants during freezing nights with the lid down and possibly sacking or some other cover over the top. Slatted shade should also be considered in case of an early heat wave.

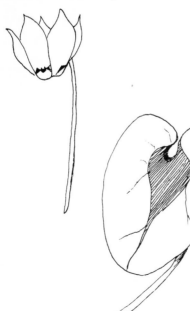

Figure 2.5
C. libanoticum

49

Cultivation

C. libanoticum, one of the most beautiful cyclamen, will flower in the open in sunny Cornwall, and reports have been heard of success out of doors in Hampshire and Kent in sheltered spots — plants have even self-sown and seeds been removed to less suitable unprepared sites by ants. Surprisingly, some of the seedlings have also flourished. However, most *libanoticum* in cultivation in cool climates are grown in pots either in a greenhouse or in a cold frame. *C. pseudibericum* will flower in pots on a sheltered patio or terrace; and *repandum* will spread by self-sown seedlings and flower prolifically in woodland. An attractive woodland walk can be set out effectively in quite a small garden. Alternatively, *repandum* may be grown in pots, and in this case pots are better than pans, since the tuber of this species survives cold winters best if it is deeply buried. Plants under shrubs and trees often come through severe frost more successfully than plants in pots in the open. Choice forms should be kept under glass, or if the weather is unusually harsh, it is advisable to take irreplaceable *repandum rhodense* or the Peloponnese forms of *repandum* into a cool room indoors. The very rare *repandum rhodense* does reasonably well on a windowsill in the house. Rooms where *Saintpaulia* thrive and flower will also be found suitable for this cyclamen. *Saintpaulia*, better known as African violets, grow naturally in shady areas of warm countries. In cultivation, they flower in the home if given a light window. The dappled shade of curtains and window frame suits them, since they need good light, but not scorching sun on the leaves. Humidity is the greatest problem indoors, as most plants require moisture in the surrounding air and central heating tends to cause a dry atmosphere. African violets are sometimes stood in bowls filled with damp peat or on wet pebbles in trays. Cyclamen can be treated in the same way, although *repandum rhodense* does not seem to object to ordinary living room temperatures and atmosphere, providing the compost is never allowed to dry out and the drainage in the pot is without fault.

Cyclamen creticum is another species which responds to extra care during the early spring and winter months. In mild seasons plants will come through to spring and flower in a sheltered place outside; but at least frame or alpine house protection is usually necessary. When the weather is bitterly cold with snow and icy winds, it is well worth making temporary arrangements to save tubers from the worst of the frost. Where there is no heating, thick layers of newspaper can be used to cover the plants; but if only a few tubers are owned, they will be safe in a cool room indoors. They are more tricky than *repandum* in the house, and should be kept cool, rather than warm. Be careful not to overwater, as growth will be slow until the spring sunshine strengthens.

In the Summer

Cyclamen purpurascens and its form *fatrense* should be flowering continuously from June onwards. Plants can be arranged together in large clay pots or groups of single pots on the patio or terrace. These summer-flowering species do seem to thrive better and thus produce more viable seed when the tubers are buried quite deeply in pots; and they benefit from the shelter of a rock or large stone in alpine gardens. In nature, and when deeply set in cultivation, tubers sometimes send flowering trunks to the surface. These floral trunks give rise to the foliage and flowers. Scented blooms follow in succession all summer. It is not wise to dry these plants off in the old-fashioned way of growing cyclamen if you wish to have evergreen, ever-flowering specimens. *C. purpurascens* has been known to flower during every month of the year, and it has been found that plants often produce less seed in a greenhouse than when grown in the open. On the other hand, in cold areas of countries with a cool climate, the flowering season can be extended by protecting the blooms from severe frost, which will damage the flowers even when foliage and tubers survive. Plants in a conservatory or glass porch remain in flower for most of the year, if not continuously, especially when they are preserved from extremes of heat and cold. However, this species is considered fully hardy and may be naturalised in large gardens: a small colony can be cultivated under shrubs and trees, where leaves will be present all year and flowers during the summer. This is useful as most of the other species do not produce leaves at the hottest time of the year.

C. graecum, usually considered as an autumn-flowering species, often flowers in late summer — when it can be induced to flower at all, because it is quite a challenge to bring plants into flower. Most growers can get their *graecum* to produce the beautiful velvety leaves, but comparatively few can make them come into bloom. The latest idea is not to dry tubers off completely; instead, they are grown in well-drained compost in deep pots, which are embedded in moist grit. This way, the long taproots can reach water, while the tuber at the top receives the necessary summer ripening of being baked by the sun. When they respond to this treatment, flowers emerge from all over the top of the tuber. Therefore, it is best to arrange *graecum* in the sunniest part of the alpine house, or if they are grown in a frame, then this should be built in a south-facing position. It might be worth considering a separate frame for the sun-loving species.

In the Autumn

The greatest number of species should be in bloom simultaneously. In most years, flowers will still be on *fatrense*, *purpurascens* and *graecum* – at least throughout the early autumn period – and other species will be full of promise with their unfolding buds. *C. hederifolium* often begins to bloom in July and by the end of summer, many plants of this species will have flowers open; naturalised *hederifolium* in churchyards and shrubberies will become a mass of pink or white colour against dark earth by August, and some flowers will not have fallen by November. Each tuber produces more flowers as it increases in size; and liquid fertiliser applied just as the flower buds begin to enlarge encourages strong, healthy stems, and maximum width of corolla and depth of colour for the species.

Naturalised *hederifolium* rarely need extra watering providing plants are growing in the shade. This is one of the species that definitely does better in the open out of doors than in a greenhouse, although a number of plants are raised under glass. Potted plants on a terrace or other paved area will require daily watering in early autumn; otherwise, the flowers will flag. Some forms of *hederifolium* bloom in late autumn, among these are the most unusual leaf patterns and plants that bear scented flowers; therefore it might be worth making or purchasing a cloche or simple frame for particular favourites, although this is not essential.

One of the first species to flower in autumn is *C. cilicium* var. *intaminatum*, followed by early-flowering forms of *hederifolium* and then typical *cilicium* with its other close relative *mirabile*. The three *cilicium* types tend to flower well if allowed more sun than *hederifolium*. They flower outside in sun or shade, but respond to the warmth of a greenhouse or glass home extension by producing more flowers and larger leaves. Plants also grow to flowering size from seed more quickly under glass, although they are perfectly hardy in the open.

As might be expected, *africanum*, although so similar to *hederifolium* in appearance, grows rapidly and flowers profusely under glass, especially if given warmth, whereas *hederifolium* quickly whithers and droops in a heated greenhouse; nevertheless, *africanum* will also wilt if not given some shade on unusually hot autumn days, as in nature it has bright light, shade from full sun and no frost.

C. rohlfsianum will come into flower early in the autumn, if situated in a warm greenhouse and kept just moist during the summer with the top of the tuber exposed to the sun. But this is a difficult species to bring into flower in the house, although not impossible on a light windowsill or in a glass extension. It is a good idea to place polythene bags over plants in the home, as this helps to maintain a humid atmosphere around the developing buds; individual pots can have small bags attached to the top with rubber bands. There is a natural resting season in the spring and early summer, when the foliage dies down. Pots should be set in moist grit or saucers of water from the middle of July to encourage new growth early in the season, as the flower buds take a number of weeks to develop to maturity by autumn. It is possible to obtain fertile seed in cultivation, and it is hoped that more people will be able to grow this fascinating species in future. In learning how to bring the plant into flower and germinate the seed of home-grown specimens, perhaps we have helped to save a very rare species from extinction: there are comparatively few *rohlfsianum* remaining in their natural habitat in Libya; in case there should be an unexpected disaster, hopefully we could reintroduce them into the wild.

Last of the autumn-flowering species is *cyprium*, last not because it is the least desirable, for it is exquisite — the pink buds open into white flowers much more finely marked with carmine at the sinus than other cyclamen — but last because it stays in flower until Christmas. Where there is no alpine house, choose a kitchen windowsill, so that you can observe the beauty and enjoy the fragrance several times a day. The species is not hardy during freezing weather, although the tubers survive in a well-constructed frame with additional newspaper coverings on cold nights, the flowers and foliage together with the season's crop of seeds might be lost if the temperature drops drastically.

In the Winter

A battle will begin to save choice plants from the ravages of wind and frost. Surprising to some, the wind does as much damage as frost to flowers, and more plants are lost from too much rain than exposure to frost. However, many gardeners must have learnt to value the winter-flowering species having watched little *coum* buds unfold after cold nights, or upon catching sight of a bed of hardy blooms all standing up straight as soon as the snow has melted. Leaves go dark while ice is on the ground from lack of water movement through the system, but they recover rapidly when the temperature begins to rise. It is possible to brush frost off plants in pots and take them to a show.

Rare forms of *coum*, such as plants which have wide silver margins or completely silvered leaves, should be given alpine house or cold frame protection, as they seem to be less hardy than the green-leaf or lightly marbled forms and they are difficult to replace.

C. parviflorum needs slightly different treatment during the flowering period. The plants are hardy; the buds emerge from the top of the tuber in September and develop slowly during late autumn. They lie flat against the tuber while the snow is on the ground and appear above soil level after Christmas, but flowers do not open fully until a period of thaw in late winter or early spring. Shade, apart from weak winter sunshine, seems to suit this dwarf species, and soil should be shallow, well-drained, peaty and always wet — summer and winter. This species thrives, flowers and seeds in cool climates. It is completely hardy and should be seen in gardens more often.

Figure 2.6
C. trochopteranthum

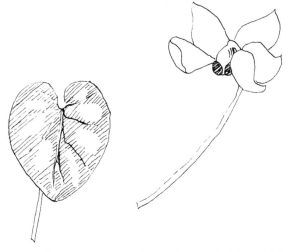

Another winter-flowering cyclamen that is suitable for growing in a cold frame is *trochopteranthum*. It can also be grown out of doors without cover, but needs a more carefully selected site than *coum*. A walled garden or a place beside the house will be found more suitable than an open bed. Most plants are grown in pots under glass, since plants are uncommon and not easy to obtain. The bold windmill or propeller-shaped flowers are delightfully fragrant, which is an added attraction and a good reason for growing some plants in the alpine house or greenhouse, where the honey scent can be appreciated.

The giant and miniature strains of *persicum*, the houseplant cyclamen, are rapidly taking over as the number one selling pot plant. A marked increase in sales has occurred since the formation of the Cyclamen Society in 1977. However, many of the plants sold as presents around Christmas time are thrown away after a short period of flowering indoors. This is a great pity, as, if they are properly treated, the tender strains of *persicum* will flower for months even in the house and still live on after spring to flower again the following season. It is not unusual to have the same plant in bloom from Christmas until Easter and bring it back into flower year after year.

C. persicum will not die at temperatures just above freezing, but without doubt plants flourish and flower better if the temperature can be kept a little higher, say around 55°F. They do best indoors when placed as near to a light window as possible in a room that has a temperature which doesn't fluctuate too quickly from very cold to very hot and vice versa. Contrary to popular opinion, tender cyclamen can be kept in the living room, especially if a fairly steady heat is maintained on every day of the week, with cooler, but not icy cold, night temperatures. Always remove plants away from a position between curtains and windows at night, remembering to replace them in the light first thing the next morning. Cyclamen can stand on a windowsill during the day even when there is snow outside; but it is when the curtains come between the pots and the room temperature after they are pulled across the windows in the evening that the danger occurs.

Water regularly, especially when cyclamen are kept in warmer rooms. It doesn't make much difference if water is applied from the top or the bottom of the pot, so long as the point where the flower stems and leaf stems meet the tuber is not allowed to get wet in the winter, otherwise rotting might spoil the plant. During very cold weather, the easiest way to water pot plants is to wait until the compost is almost dry and then stand the pot in a bowl of lukewarm water for a couple of hours. The ideal is to keep the compost just moist all the time: it shouldn't be soaking wet or dust dry, but like a nicely squeezed out dish-cloth. This is tricky to get just right, but the technique of watering houseplants comes with practice, and once this skill has been mastered, especially with cyclamen, the number of losses will be greatly reduced. Plants that have been allowed to flag due to lack of watering can be revived if the pots are stood in a bucket of tepid water, but never leave cyclamen continuously standing in water for days, as good drainage is essential.

Houseplant strains of *persicum* even tolerate central heating if some provision is made for creating a humid atmosphere: one method is to stand pots on trays containing pebbles. The pebbles are kept wet and moist air rises around the foliage. It is worth trying more than one strain of this species, since some are more adaptable to the light and air of living rooms than others.

In the greenhouse, maintain a steady temperature of around 55°F for this species, and see that there is adequate ventilation. Pick off dead blooms and generally keep the bench as clean as possible to discourage insects and other pests such as slugs. Water regularly, taking care not to overwater, and pick out moss and weeds.

Winter-flowering species in flower in an unheated alpine house can be given added protection if an empty glass or a plastic jam or honey jar is temporarily inverted over the choice specimens when sudden drops in the temperature occur, but try not to leave these in place longer than absolutely necessary. At every opportunity remove mouldy flowers and attempt to keep the tops of tubers dry with a grit top dressing. However, the leaves of cyclamen need a humid atmosphere so avoid dry heat. Thawing after frost should be natural and slow, not by removing plants to a warm room.

Typical forms of *coum* will have their buds ready to open before Christmas and come into full bloom when the snow melts. They will stay in flower in the open garden through the coldest months until March, and by this time the spring-flowering species will be ready to take over the floral display. (See also Chapter 4.)

<table>
<tr><td>Care of the
Resting Tuber</td><td>

Dormancy is characteristic of cyclamen: in some species the dormant period has been drastically reduced or overcome altogether, due to man's intervention and eagerness to have flowering plants from seed in the minimum time possible; in other species, a period of dormancy is an essential part of the ripening process.

</td></tr>
</table>

First, all seedlings should be kept growing continuously after germination, as resting during the one-leaf or cotyledon stage is often fatal. It is now fairly easy to keep *persicum* growing on successfully in a warm greenhouse, but other species can be troublesome.

If small tubers have swollen with stored food and water during their first autumn and winter, and the leaves have been healthy and green all that time, then when they begin to disappear one by one towards mid-summer, this is quite natural and no harm should come to the resting tuber.

Hardy types may be left in the frame, patio pot, terrace bed or rockery throughout summer. Labels in pots and markers in beds will be found more than useful, since if many species and forms are grown, or where cyclamen are planted in beds with other bulbs, they not only identify the names of the individual forms, but they warn the gardener not to dig over certain patches, when no sign of life is visible above ground. And it is important to remember that growth begins again by the first weeks in July below ground. If the places where cyclamen are planted should be very dry, start regular watering again at this time.

Little or no water, other than natural rainfall, will be required by resting tubers out of doors during June. But note that *fatrense* and *purpurascens* are evergreen and cannot be classed as resting tubers in summer, when they are coming into bloom. There is no true resting period for all the forms of *purpurascens*. However, *parviflorum*, the little winter-flowering *coum* type of cyclamen, is also exceptional: the leaves die back as in other hardy cyclamen, until none are left by June, but the roots continue to remain active and require water during every month of the year. Top growth begins early in the season (mid- to late summer) but development is so slow at first that leaf and flower buds are not seen above soil level for months. Tubers should be kept moist at all times. This species can take more water and wetter compost than the other species, but the rule for good drainage still holds.

Where species *balearicum, cilicium* and varieties, *mirabile, coum* and varieties, *creticum, hederifolium, pseudibericum, repandum* and *trochopteranthum* are grown in a cold frame, keep only just moist in summer. Pots sunk in grit, pebbles or sand are better not watered from above during mid-summer – water will be absorbed from below if the area surrounding the pots is watered. Take special care to see that pots are not over-watered, or water-logged; otherwise, resting tubers making little or no growth will rot: as many precious plants are lost this way, as by frost damage in winter. Rest these species in dappled shade.

Species *africanum, cyprium, graecum, libanoticum, persicum* and *rohlfsianum* require different treatment during the warm months. *C. africanum* on a sunny greenhouse or alpine house bench will quite likely remain in growth until almost the next season with only a very short rest at the end of June, and by the time the last leaves fall, the new leaf buds will be visible at the top of the tuber. The leaves appear with the flowers.

Cyclamen which came originally from warmer countries get the good ripening they need if pots are placed in a sunny south-facing frame with the lid only just raised. Some species require more sun in summer than others, for example *repandum rhodense* does best in a frame which receives some sun and some shade in summer.

Pots containing species that ripen well with a sun-baking in summer may also be left on the greenhouse bench, where they will lose all their leaves by June. The greatest danger at this time is from rotting due to over-wet compost. Resting species will be without leaves for several weeks and it can be difficult to determine when regular watering should commence again for the new season. About the middle of July, stone chippings can be gently tipped into the hand so that the tops of tubers can be examined for flower buds; but even if there is no new growth, water can be given sparingly to prevent tubers from shrivelling.

The houseplant strains of *persicum* are best not dried off completely. The reason why many people lose their plants during the summer is because they fail to get tubers back into growth after leaving them for months without water. Gardeners used to leave pots on their sides under the greenhouse bench during the resting season; but modern nurseries do not allow the compost to become too dry. Watering is still reduced as the foliage gradually dies down after flowering, but not stopped altogether.

Where just a few houseplant cyclamen are grown, the best method of bringing them back into flower is to keep pots in a place where they receive sunshine for half of the day; leave the tops of the tubers exposed so that they can have a baking and reduce watering so that the compost is moist rather than wet. Top-dress with fresh compost at the beginning of July, and from the middle of the month until the middle of August, new season flower buds will begin to appear on the floral trunks or simply from odd knobs anywhere on the flat top of the tuber. New leaves will begin to appear about the same time. Tender young leaves need some form of shade during heat wave periods. Pots may be stood directly on the patio or terrace paving if no greenhouse or frame is available; but keep a sharp look out for caterpillars, slugs and snails. Pick pots up regularly to make sure they are not being attacked by pests which hide during the daytime.

Occasionally a tuber of any species will fail to come into growth for a whole year but remain firm and healthy. In other words, although showing no sign of softness or hollowness, leaves and roots remain dormant on a tuber which appears to be sound but lifeless. These tubers should be watered moderately during the natural growing period for the species. Then try standing the pot in a pan containing 5 cm depth of water with a polythene bag secured to the top of the pot. Loosen the polythene once a day to allow fresh air to enter. Summer- and autumn-flowering species seem to miss a year more often than winter- and spring-flowering species, and greenhouse grown plants more often than outdoor grown plants. The phenomenon occurs fairly frequently in *cilicium*, *graecum* and *persicum*. Quite possibly not enough water is given to rouse them from the resting state. However, too much water with insufficient drainage when tubers are dormant will cause rotting.

CHAPTER 3

Propagation

Nearly all cyclamen plants come from seed. The best time to sow is as soon as the capsules are ripe: this varies from species to species and year to year, depending slightly on the weather. The summer-flowering species take a whole year, from one summer until the next, whereas the winter- and spring-flowering species develop after flowering until late summer of the same year — only a few months. For example, seed of *C. purpurascens* is sometimes ready to sow by mid-summer, and most of the other species ripen slowly through the summer towards autumn. Capsules of *pseudibericum* are usually the last to mature.

Sowing Seed of Hardy Species

It is characteristic of the genus that the capsule coils down to soil level after fertilisation has taken place. The tiny fruit then takes months to turn into the mature pea-sized capsule carrying ripe seeds. (It has been found that grit, small pebbles or limestone chippings placed around the parent plants at the top of pots help to keep the pedicels dry and so preserves them from rotting during this long period from pollination to ripe capsule.) The capsule is ready to split if the skin gives under gentle pressure of the thumb or fingers and the colour is going brown. When the seed can be seen glistening brown in its surrounding jelly-like mucilage within the skin once it has split and peeled back, gather the harvest and sow. If the seeds are sown when they are still fresh and sticky, successful germination is more likely to result.

If left to nature, it is most likely that seed of each species will germinate during the season that the parent bears foliage, although there is a lot of overlap and late autumn is the main germinating time in a cool climate. *C. hederifolium* often begins to sprout before *cilicium*, followed by other autumn species and then *coum* types begin to appear after November. Seed that is not gathered will self-sow and seedlings are found around the pots, or plants in beds, wherever they fall; and birds and ants remove them quite a distance, even up the steep sides of tubs and large containers. (It is curious that germination can be so erratic: *coum* seed has been known to germinate many years after being sown and *repandum* regularly stays dormant for more than a year.)

If old seed is being used, a good soaking in ordinary tap water for a day or two is advantageous. The seed swells to several times its original size after soaking and the outer seed coat changes colour. Although most hardy cyclamen are sown in the late summer and early autumn, some nurseries are so busy at this time, that they are more or less obliged to sow later in the year.

Cyclamen sown in summer and autumn should germinate the same winter, but patience is needed as the first leaves take several weeks to appear. Frost action seems to aid germination of the hardiest species.

A 20 cm diameter pot or pan is ideal for the rarer species, where comparatively small quantities of seed are available, bearing in mind that seedlings are best left undisturbed for over a year and tiny pots dry out too quickly. Large trays may be used for the commoner forms of *coum* and *hederifolium*, but sow singly with a small pair of tweezers. The seed of all the species is large enough to handle easily, so there is no need to scatter carelessly, one seed on top of another, as with dust-fine seed of other types of plants, where separation of the seeds is nearly impossible. Some gardeners recommend mixing the seed with sand to make handling even easier, but I have not found this necessary.

Choose a light, airy seed compost; although it is better to err on the side of too well-drained rather than too colloidal, an extremely open soil dries out within the day in spring. A suitable compost can be mixed as follows: 2 parts peat; one part course grit with sand; one part limestone chippings and one part John Innes. The limestone neutralises some of the acidity in the peat and this helps to keep the soil sweet. A properly balanced mixture feels right when a handful is run through the fingers. There is no sticky feel and the colour is dark brown contrasting with the light stone.

An alternative is to put seeds into once-used potting compost. The first crop, such as annual seedlings or bedding plant cuttings, removes dusty particles which can clog the cyclamen seedling roots.

As mentioned in the last chapter, the pot should be prepared by covering the drainage hole with a piece of perforated zinc. Next, a handful of chippings or small pebbles goes into the bottom, followed by a trowel of the airy compost mixture. Put seed still covered with the mucilage straight from the capsule into a thin layer of dry silver sand, and cover the seed with a layer of compost. Spread 2.5 cm of stone chippings on top and give the pot a thorough watering.

The next stage often makes all the difference between good

germination and only one or two isolated seedlings emerging from their hard seed-coats: small pots are encased in polythene bags to keep in the moisture, which definitely aids germination. Twist or tie the necks to prevent drying out, but open the bags at regular intervals to let in fresh air. Large trays may be covered with a sheet of glass, which serves the same purpose as the polythene: it keeps in moisture. Turn the glass every day and there will be no need to water again between sowing and germination, as seed should be damp not wet. Don't forget to label as you go. Summer and autumn sowings will germinate in a shady cold frame or simply in pots or trays placed outside against a north-facing wall or fence. The hardy species can spend their first winter in a bulb frame: some will be ready for planting out in flowerbeds the following summer; others can stay in the frame or be moved to tubs and window boxes.

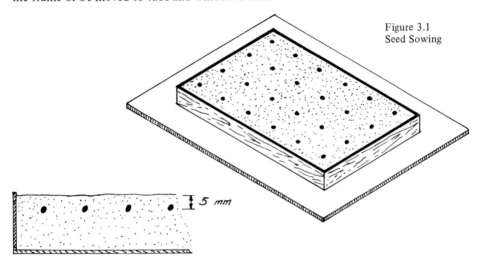

Figure 3.1
Seed Sowing

5 mm

Germination Tests

Two trays of mixed seeds were sown on 5 September as an experiment and further control was provided by a similar sowing in pots. The trays contained two rows of *coum* (common forms of *album* and *roseum*); one row of *hederifolium* 'Bowles' Apollo'; one row of variegated *intaminatum*; two rows of *balearicum*; one row of fragrant *hederifolium* and one row of a pure breeding *coum album*. The compost used was the home-made mixture described above.

One tray was sown and covered in the usual way. Tray number two was sown in the same order but the seed was left exposed. The tray top-dressed with limestone grit was covered with a sheet of glass and placed in an unheated greenhouse. The tray with the seeds exposed was also covered with a sheet of glass, then placed on paving which receives early morning sun filtered through leaves — an almost completely shady site. Small pots were sown with the same species of seed and half were covered and half left uncovered. The 5 mm covering of compost was left without the stone chippings topping on some pots as an extra test. All the seed had been soaked in tap water for several days before sowing.

Results. The *hederifolium* (both fragrant and 'Bowles' Apollo') was the first seed to germinate and this was in the tray placed in shade outside. The white radicles were seen pushing out of the seed-coats at the beginning of November. *C. intaminatum* followed a week later also in the tray outside. Those species in pots covered with chippings germinated well about the same time, but it was more difficult to observe the exact time the seed-coats split under the stone chippings. *C. coum* germinated at the beginning of December out of doors.

Figure 3.2
The Developing
Seedling

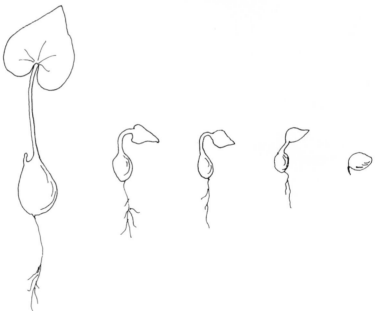

The results of the experiment show that hardy cyclamen germinate readily in cool, shady places. *C. hederifolium* sown earlier, in July, were sprouting all over a tray as successfully as mustard and cress, and these were coming through a generous covering of stone chippings. The tray sown in September without chippings soon began to go green as various mosses started to grow, whereas the tray and the pots with chippings stayed clear all winter.

In the greenhouse, germination of the seed in the experimental trays was less successful. A pot was stood on the glass when space was short and the first seedlings appeared in the extra shade that this provided, proving once again that shade is necessary for

Figure 3.3
C. persicum,
Large-flowering
Cultivated Variety

germination of cyclamen seed. A sheet of paper placed on top of the glass is beneficial for trays kept in a glasshouse. Many times seedlings of all the species have been found growing in the damp shade along the inside of the base below the glass, where it is semi-dark and constantly moist.

It should be remembered that some of the species need more warmth than others for germination. *Cyclamen libanoticum* germinates at living room temperatures: seed sown the last week of September began to sprout the first week in November; and seed of the tender strains of *persicum* will germinate at any time of year if kept moist at a temperature of between 60° and 68°F in the dark.

Seed Sowing – Tender persicum

August sowings of the florists' strains of *persicum* can be germinated in a cold frame to flower on large plants before Christmas 15 months later. Alternatively, to gain smaller flowering plants nine months later, sow in January and February at about 65°F. If an early maturing strain is chosen it is even possible to sow at the beginning of March in order to have plants in full bloom for Christmas.

Soak seed for two days and sow in John Innes or soil-less compost, spacing the seed 5 cm apart and 5 mm deep. Remember to keep the compost watered at all times after sowing, as it is important that the seed should not be allowed to dry. A covering of glass topped with a sheet of brown paper to keep the compost moist until germination has been found helpful. An alternative method for *persicum*, which is practised commercially, is to add a layer of peat after sowing. This aids water retention and is removed when the cotyledons have emerged. It can be brushed off without disturbing the compost underneath.

Raising Young Plants – Hardy Species

Most seedlings develop one cotyledon, or seed-leaf, but occasionally two are produced. Certainly, if the first single cotyledon is damaged another follows in most cases. The seed-leaf is different in shape from the true leaves; it is usually more heart-shaped, often a lighter colour and has a dull rather than a shiny surface.

In about a year, the seedling tubers are tiny white balls of water with a thin skin. At that stage it can be tricky pricking them out, as the minute root or shoot is easily damaged. It is safer when plants are coming back into growth in the second year. The tubers are not much bigger but they are slightly stronger and beginning to turn a colour. When the hard skin has formed, each tuber is better able to stand disturbance and future dormant periods without shrivelling to the point of no recovery.

During the first year, it is almost impossible to over-water

64

Plate 1 (*above*). *C. persicum* 'Victoria'

Plate 2 (*below*). *C. coum* around a rose bed

Plate 3 (*above*). *C. libanoticum.*

Plate 4 (*below*). *C. parviflorum.*

Plate 5 (*above*). *C. balearicum*

Plate 6 (*below*). *C. pseudibericum*

Plate 7 (*above*). *C. repandum*

Plate 8 (*left*). *C. purpurascens*

Plate 9 (*below*). *C. graecum album*

Plate 10 (*above*). *C. cyprium*

Plate 11 (*above*). *C. rohlfsianum*

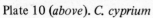

Plate 12 *(below)*. *C. Purpurascens*

Plate 13 (*left*). *C. mirabile*

Plate 14 (*above*). *C. hederifolium*

Plate 15 (*left*). *C. cilium* var. *intaminatum*

Plate 16 (*above*). *C. trochopteranthum*

Plate 17 (*right*). *C. creticum*

Plate 18 (*above*). *C. africanum*

Plate 19 (*left*). Old flower card

seedlings, as long as pots or trays are well-drained. Always keep young plants in the shade.

Prick off *persicum* seedlings at the two-leaf stage. Note that the tiny tuber is planted so that the top is exposed and not buried as in the hardy species. Buy or make up a good potting compost. Soil-less compost may be used or John Innes No. 1. Space plants 7.5 cm apart in trays or plant individually in 7.5 cm pots.

A temperature of 55° to 60°F should be maintained until the roots fill the pots and the leaves nearly touch on the trays. The area where the plants are growing needs to be shaded from fierce sunshine, but not so shady that the petioles lengthen.

Six weeks after the seedlings are pricked out, they should be ready to move on again. Take extra care regarding the depth of planting, as experiments have shown that tubers covered with compost are slow to produce flowering buds and more leaves appear. The stems easily rot when the tubers are buried.

If the temperature is low (around 55°F) in early September, this encourages flower bud production. Plants will need all the autumn light available in cool climates; otherwise small leaves with long petioles reaching for the light will be the result.

It is interesting that temperature effects both flower and bud growth but in different ways: more leaves develop and rapid foliage growth occurs when higher temperatures are maintained and more flower bud growth occurs when the lower temperature is introduced. Lower temperatures also reduce leaf development; so to some extent flowers are produced at the expense of leaves and vice versa. Therefore to gain the best results, pay careful attention to sunlight and temperature. A hot, dry atmosphere is not suitable for young cyclamen plants: aim at warmth and shade for germination and very young seedlings; sun but not blazing sunshine during the growing on stage in summer; full light and cool surroundings to encourage flower bud production in the autumn.

Regular feeding with liquid fertiliser is highly beneficial from the time the seedlings are moved to their first pots, and then again two weeks later and continuously until the final potting stage; then from two weeks later until flowering.

One of the great advantages of giving away seedlings or young plants to gardening friends, besides the joy of being able to grant someone the pleasure of flowering a beautiful plant, is the insurance of preserving the cultivar, form or strain. This works particularly well in the case of rare plant material. Many a gardener has been pleased to be offered the return of seeds from an offspring, or a rooted cutting, when the original plant has been lost by accident or a gamble with the weather.

Taking Cuttings
or Dividing
the Tuber

Cyclamen are propagated by seed as this is by far the easiest method. However, vegetative propagation is not impossible, although it rarely occurs in nature — perhaps never. Possibly a small portion of a tuber sometimes becomes detached and roots itself in surrounding soil in the wild, much the same way as a broken potato with an 'eye' or part of a dahlia would develop roots in the right environment.

In cultivation, cuttings are taken in slightly varying ways, according to the plant material available. The most suitable plants for vegetative propagation are those which have already started the process, i.e. in nature, some cyclamen produce a structure known as a floral trunk. This forms in several shapes; but the most common are knobbly structures found at the centre top or as an extension of the parent tuber from the side.

In the wild, seeds frequently germinate on the platform at the top of the tuber. This can happen year after year, so that offspring of one, two, three, four or more years are all clustered over the parent — the new foliage of the offspring blocks the light from the foliage of the old plant. For survival, the original cyclamen develops a trunk which rises above all the foliage of subsequent generations of offspring. New foliage and flowers grow from the top of the trunk.

Floral trunks have been found on *africanum*, *graecum*, *hederifolium*, *purpurascens* and *persicum* and short branching trunks on *coum* and *cyprium*. Trunks of up to 30 cm or more in length appear on *graecum*, even in pots; but normally they form on plants that have tubers deeply buried under rocks.

Floral trunks on *persicum* are often short, arched and covered with flower buds. Older plants develop floral trunks, but they are not often found on specimens flowering in their first or second year. This species also produces new islands of growth at the side: a small cluster of leaves and flowers will develop on one side or both sides of a large plant. Upon investigation, by knocking the plant gently out of the pot, it will be seen that however much the roots seem to come from the islands, in fact, when all the soil is brushed away, the roots can be seen quite clearly to be growing from the main tuber. In other words, the new islands of foliage and flowers emerge from extensions of the parent plant which are not detached and self-supporting. They seem like plantlets because of their position at the sides and because several can form round one parent tuber in the manner of offspring, but they are short lateral floral trunks. If it was known how to induce the production of this type of floral trunk, vegetative reproduction would be easier and large-scale commercial

66

cultivar introduction simplified. (Commercial vegetative reproduction might also be developed by the use of cotyledon cuttings.)

Most gardeners can raise plants successfully from floral trunks. Dip the tuber end of the cutting in hormone rooting powder straight away. Pot up the floral trunk and place a polythene bag over the pot, securing with a rubber band to hold in moisture during the period that roots are forming. Place in a bulb frame or shady part of a greenhouse.

To propagate by dividing the parent tuber, or separating a lateral floral trunk, slice off a section with at least one healthy leaf, preferably two or more. Pass the raw wound of the parent cyclamen over a flame to cauterise and then coat with candle wax to seal the surface area. Dip the raw surface of the lateral floral trunk in hormone rooting powder, or, if a large section is taken, cauterise and seal as before.

Protect rooting plants from bright sun and water sparingly; the polythene bag treatment prevents loss of turgidity in the leaves. Late spring and early autumn are good times to attempt vegetative reproduction. But even in the hands of experienced gardeners it is a slow job and there is a danger that both parent and cuttings might be lost, therefore this form of reproduction is not recommended if the plant is irreplaceable.

One of the purposes of attempting to root cyclamen from cuttings is to try and obtain more specimens identical to a particularly choice plant that appears in a batch of seedlings. This cannot be done by sowing seed, as the plant will not necessarily breed true if propagated sexually, although after many generations of controlled pollination a strain will come almost 100 per cent true from seed and a cultivar name becomes a possibility.

CHAPTER 4

Where to Grow Cyclamen

The Alpine House

The main difference between an alpine house and an ordinary greenhouse is that the former is usually built with a row of windows all the way along the roof and extra ventilators are included on the sides. Ventilation is of utmost importance when growing alpines, as tiny plants are soon lost if moulds damage roots or leaves.

The windows in an alpine house are kept open even in the winter. Most alpine plants are hardy and will survive frost. Many species of cyclamen are hardy, but some are only just hardy and protection is given during bitterly cold weather, either by giving enough heat to prevent frost or, more often, by placing mats, newspapers or polythene over the tender plants during icy weather.

It should be remembered that potted cyclamen are more likely to be lost during frost than plants buried in the ground. This can be counteracted to some extent by burying the pots up to their necks in pebbles or gritty sand on the benches. The grit also helps to keep the compost in the pots moist but not too wet.

Plants which come from high mountain areas have long winter rests under the snow and put up their exquisite flowers after the ice melts in spring. During the time they are under the snow, they are cold and dry, not cold and wet, therefore the combination of overwatering and cold is damaging. If pots are well-drained, hardy cyclamen stand quite low temperatures. It is when plants are waterlogged that tubers are lost: winter rains on plants in the open are more harmful than the cold. Thus, although hardy cyclamen can be grown outside with simply a sheet of glass, or more elaborately a bulb frame to keep off excess water, the advantages of an alpine house are many.

Plants that go well with cyclamen in an alpine house include the closely related primulas. The carmine colour of *C. pseudibericum* contrasts magnificently with the lavender-blue primrose-shaped flowers of *Primula marginata* 'Linda Pope'. The *marginata* refers to

68

the splendid leaves, which look as though they have been cut with pinking scissors and edged with silver dust. They remain on the plant for most of the year, smelling of incense and reducing to fat buds at the end of winter just before they start to uncurl and put up their flowers in spring. Another *marginata*, called 'Pritchard's Variety' with not such blue flowers and not such broad leaves, is also worth having in an alpine house to contrast with cyclamen in the spring.

Other primulas and auriculas might also be considered. *Primula farinosa* with minute fairy-pink flowers and *P. allionii* with bold pink short-stemmed flowers that come in bright clusters; auriculas with black flowers and green margins to the petals; yellow auricula 'Queen Alexandra' with a sweet scent and frilly margin; clear blue auriculas, and some with silver dust all over the foliage. There are also uncommon cultivated forms with names that suit them, such as 'Gnome' for one with pillar-box red flowers. Strangely even the brightly coloured alpines seem to harmonise with the pastel pinks of spring cyclamen. It is not often that natural colours clash in the alpine house.

The spring-flowering silver saxifrages are handsome plants. The earliest flowering species are a constant joy, like the rare *Saxifraga crystallae*; or *S. grisebachii* – a fantastic plant with an odd-looking turkey-neck inflorescence which rises up from the centre of the silver rosette in February. At first bright crimson, it gradually extends to 17.5 cm before opening into pink bell-flowers that are insignificant when compared to the feathery peduncle. Later in the year, there is a saxifrage to keep the summer-flowering *Cyclamen purpurascens* company. 'Tumbling Waters' is as beautiful as it sounds. The rosette of strap-like leaves encrusted with silver sends up an amazing inflorescence of flowers that truly resemble a waterfall. There is also a tiny saxifrage *minutaefolia* which forms a cushion of rosettes.

Amongst the primulas and the saxifrages in an alpine house, small bulbs will bloom in their seasons. In early spring, *Crocus*, *Narcissus* and *Iris* species. *Narcissus junctifolius* has an interesting fragrance and blooms at the same time as some of the less hardy cyclamen in April and May. In late spring, the rather weird *Albuca* will follow with its white and green flowers like a cross between a snowdrop and a crocus.

In the alpine house in autumn and winter, cyclamen are so choice and rare, especially the scented species, that they often seem more valuable than at other times of the year. If such delicate treasures are left to compete with creeping and trailing plants in the open, even if able to withstand the weather, they sometimes lose the battle for survival.

The 'Mixed'
House

It may be that you enjoy growing other plants besides alpines and wonder if you could include some cyclamen amongst your various crops.

If you have a small greenhouse, it is most likely that in spring the shelves are crammed with seed-trays full of annuals, half-hardy biennials and perennials for the summer display in the garden. Zonal pelargoniums and begonias probably fill most of the space above ground level with perhaps tomatoes, cucumbers and capsicums growing upwards from rooting bags underneath. It is even possible that a few favourite cacti are fitted in somewhere and bowls of bulbs in spring and autumn. But unless there is heat, the mixed house is almost certainly rather bleak in winter.

Cyclamen can change that. They can be grown surprisingly well with other plants, allowing for a little ingenuity in the gardener. In the late autumn, winter and early spring, when most species are flowering, they can have the greenhouse almost to themselves and the hardy species will provide decoration without requiring expensive heating.

Seedlings and young plants can be grown outside along the base of a shady wall during late spring and summer, when space is wanted for bedding plants and salad fruits; and when it is time for the less hardy cyclamen to come inside again, the tomatoes will be ready for harvesting. But don't leave it too late, or the best *africanum* or *cyprium* is sure to suffer damage, which will show as a mushy tuber a few days or weeks later. The last green fruits of the tomatoes can be ripened indoors on trays. There is no need to wrap them, or hide them in the dark, they turn red if arranged on trays in the garage or on a windowsill in the house. The old stems should be removed immediately so that the greenhouse is left clean and tidy for the cold months.

Reserve a small area in the mixed house for the species of cyclamen that need a summer ripening, unless there is a bulb frame where they could be kept from April until August; either way, leave watering instructions against the plants if you go away, as care with species that are resting is important: *cyprium* and *libanoticum* will receive no water in mid-summer; *africum* and *persicum* will be given little water, and *graecum* and *rohlfsianum* only the moisture from the sand surrounding the pots.

It is even possible to grow a small selection of the tender house-plant strains of *persicum* in an unheated mixed house, if early-maturing types are chosen and the whole operation is carried out from March until October. The seeds will need artificial heat for germination, but a propagator can be used, or a single tray can be kept in an airing cupboard with a polythene bag to keep in the moisture. Seedlings should be transferred to the greenhouse as soon as the danger of frost has passed, and young plants can be moved outside for the summer months, when geraniums and other plants in the mixed house are flowering, or tomatoes and green peppers take all the space. When the buds are well up on the cyclamen in October, they can be taken to a cool room in the house. In some areas, where cold nights come in September, they will have to go back under glass for a few weeks before coming indoors. They should be in full flower by Christmas. If more than a few plants of *persicum* are grown, part of the greenhouse can be sectioned off and heated with electricity; but the temperature should not drop below 45°F and 50-55°F is preferable.

Where the purchase of a greenhouse is to be a new venture, choose a glass-to-ground design, as this will give the most growing space. Several hardy species of cyclamen flourish in the shade and these will grow under the bench, if this is the only space that can be spared.

However, where cyclamen are grown, remember to ventilate the greenhouse summer and winter. It is not possible to preserve warmth simply by keeping the windows shut. Cyclamen will die if they are situated for long periods where the air is not circulating. Of course the windows may be closed during frosty nights and on days when the frost doesn't lift from morning until night; but it is best to open the windows as often as the temperature is above freezing.

A Cyclamen Greenhouse

If you wish to specialise in hardy cyclamen, an alpine house as described could be used for all the species and rare forms of this one genus and no other plants. In this case, arrange the plants so that the species that require a ripening in the sun are at the sunniest end of the house, e.g. *graecum*; those that benefit from moderate sun are in the middle, e.g. *cilicium*, and those that do well in warm shade are on the shady side of the house, or on the floor, e.g. *balearicum*. *Cyclamen hederifolium*, all forms of *coum* and *parviflorum* thrive in cool shade.

Sometimes moving pots from one part of a greenhouse to another makes the difference between a poor specimen that never seems to grow and a flourishing plant that produces healthy leaves and masses of bloom. Experiment with your own cyclamen to find the best light for each species; but refrain from moving them so often that they never get a chance to acclimatise: plants adapt slowly to change.

If the greenhouse is to be just for tender *persicum* a wide range of colours in several strains could be chosen. A house full of the newer miniature hybrids might be considered, or a mixture of these with some of the better large-flowering florists' strains — the pure whites and plain colours; and one section could be reserved for flowers with frilled and fimbriated corollas; another for silver and beautifully marbled foliage. A few novelties such as double flowers or striped petals could be included; but at least a small space should be kept for the wild species from Cyprus and Tunisia and for cultivated plants like these with scented flowers.

Figure 4.1
C. cilicium

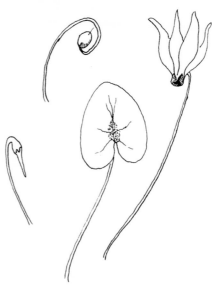

The temperature of the greenhouse must be kept above freezing during the winter. An electric propagator will greatly facilitate germination and make it possible to maintain high temperatures for seedlings during the cold months, as no doubt the *Cyclamen persicum* enthusiast will wish to sow in August and again in January and March in order to try early maturing and late maturing types — especially if enormous plants in large pots are required for shows and small pots with scented flowers are used to decorate windowsills and tables at Christmas time. By following a strict routine of sowing and potting on in sequence it is possible to have flowers on *persicum* all the year round in a heated greenhouse or a light room. (See also Chapter 6.)

Cyclamen in the Home

Cyclamen are now more popular as houseplants. Since the introduction of the new mini-strain, which was developed especially for windowsills, there has been an increase in the sales of small plants in small pots. A plant in a 7.5 cm container is expected to carry up to two hundred flowers and stay in bloom for many months in the living room. The older large-flowering strains were less tolerant of the varying temperatures found in the average home.

Thousands of cyclamen come on to the market every autumn:

the peak selling period is still during the months before Christmas. Large pots of cyclamen are still given as presents, but the increasing popularity of the mini-cyclamen has extended the selling period right up until Easter.

Plants sold in small pots at the beginning of the autumn season are mostly produced from seed sown at the beginning of the year. Another batch of seed is sown for flowers at Christmas; and the latest idea is to have plants in full bloom in the summer — by choosing special varieties this is now a possibility. Early flowering is achieved by paying careful attention to sowing dates, liquid feeding, transplanting at the correct time and by providing the right amount of light. It also helps to select varieties which do especially well during different seasons.

In Pots

Where is the best place to put cyclamen in the house? In a modern home where the heat is thermostatically controlled so that every room has more or less the same temperature, the only consideration will be light. Try to place pots on a windowsill rather than in a dark alcove. A table near patio doors or glass-to-floor windows will be suitable, and an indoor flowerbed built near the light is very effective. Avoid a position that is close to a radiator, although if the radiators are under the windows, it is possible to keep cyclamen on the ledges if pots are sunk in outer containers filled with peat which is kept moist.

In houses where different temperatures are maintained according to the number of rooms in use, choose a light, *cool* room. The flowers last longest in a light, airy place but the petioles will soon lengthen in hot, dark rooms. When the leaf-stems are long and thin with small leaves bending towards the light, the plants lose their attractive, compact appearance.

Leaves often go yellow on cyclamen because the gift-plant is so precious that it is over-watered. It is best to water pots well and then wait until the compost is beginning to go dry before watering again. However, don't wait until it is actually dry, as the leaves will certainly go yellow.

Liquid fertiliser may be given regularly while the gift-plant is still healthy and producing new buds and leaves. The fertiliser should be diluted according to the manufacturer's instructions and never given to a specimen which is losing all its foliage, or there will be a chemical build-up in the compost, which won't do the ailing plant any good.

As the flowers fade, pull them out gently with the stalk attached, right from the tuber. Also remove any dead leaves in the same way, taking care not to tug so hard that an adjoining bud comes away too.

(Incidentally, it is possible to ripen seed capsules on quite a shady windowsill in the house, if required — afternoon sunshine will be sufficient.)

In cool rooms, make sure the top of the tuber is raised above compost level, since if the tuber is completely covered with soil, rotting of the base of flower and leaf stems is difficult to prevent. This is more important in winter than summer.

In Window Boxes

The species *hederifolium* is suitable for a box in the shade. It is a labour-saving choice, as once the tubers are planted little further attention is required. The occasional weeding, an annual top-dressing with bone-meal, and a liquid feed now and then, as the flower buds come out, will be all that is necessary. Advantages include the long autumn flowering season plus attractive foliage for every month of the year, except June.

Figure 4.2
Hardy Species Grow
Well in Window
Boxes

Winter is a time when some boxes are left empty. If small pots of *coum* are buried in the compost of the box, they can be set in place after the summer display of bedding plants, such as petunias, finishes in autumn. Polyanthus followed by *Impatiens*, followed by *coum* is another idea for a box in the semi-shade.

Lots of *purpurascens* in a box beneath a window that catches the morning sun will suit the gardener who likes fragrant flowers close to the house in summer. Where there is a box facing south, *graecum* might thrive — if the depth allows for the long roots — although success with this species is more likely if the box is under a balcony or has some other form of shelter to protect the plants from too much rain.

In Flower Arrangements

Cyclamen make excellent cut flowers. And now that the mini-cyclamen are being bred with so many flowers per plant, the use of cyclamen is not as extravagant as it might seem. In Germany, they are illustrated in vases in the catalogues.

The flowers should be pulled from the tuber and the end of the stem cut back slightly with a sharp knife, preferably at an oblique angle, to allow the stalk to take up water more efficiently. The blooms live for up to a month in water, and remain fresh and keep their colour for most of that time.

There are many colours and types of bloom, and no other plant provides a better white flower than cyclamen. They can be arranged attractively on their own or with other delicate flowers. A charming display for a table decoration consists of a shallow bowl of lilac or mauve double *Colchicum* with pale pink or white autumn-flowering cyclamen. The cultivated strains of *persicum* have turgid flower stalks, which can be pushed into 'Oasis' blocks quite easily for more formal arrangements.

Neat collections of plants can be grown on paving close to the house, or tender cyclamen can be grouped attractively in wooden tubs in heated home extensions. Several small pots sunk in a tub of peat will be easier to manage than plants tipped from their individual containers.

Cyclamen on the Terrace or Patio

Cyclamen are particularly suitable for the patio because they are small. They can be lifted and replanted at almost any time of year, or pots can be buried in patio beds to replace summer bedding plants that have stopped flowering. Species can be found that will flower in sun or shade, alkaline or acid soil, in any kind of container (with drainage holes) and during every season.

In the enclosed environment of a patio, the hardy species may be arranged in pots, tubs and boxes; and some of the less hardy species can be tried: *africanum*, *balearicum*, *graecum* and *libanoticum* might survive if the patio is very sheltered. *C. graecum* and *libanoticum* have been known to come through the winter out of doors in cool climates against a south-facing sunny wall or bank.

Hardy cyclamen can be planted in outdoor tubs. Good results have been obtained from growing the summer-flowering *purpurascens*, planted deeply in the soil of the tub. They grew into large tubers, which were much more floriferous than similar plants in small pots, and they set plenty of seed. Other species such as *hederifolium*, *cilicium* and *coum* do well in tubs.

Choose the hardiest species for terraces. All the species suggested in the rockery section will be suitable for a bed at the boundary wall of a terrace. A selection of winter-, spring-, summer- and autumn-flowering species will give constant joy. It is a good idea to mix the species and the varieties if the bed is large enough to take a number of plants, to provide year-round colour and interest; but try to arrange them in small groups of each kind rather than one plant of each species, as this gives a more natural effect, which is more pleasing.

If the terrace bed is against the house, the wall will provide some protection and a little warmth, and tend to be drier than a similar bed in the open. Keep this bed for rare and uncommon cyclamen. Unusual forms of *coum* can go at the foot of the wall on the shady side, where they are likely to thrive and multiply.

Cyclamen in the Small Garden

Cyclamen look lovely in drifts, but they are equally at home in terrace pots, in raised beds or between paving slabs in small gardens. They are particularly suitable for enchanting country cottage gardens and the tiny paved areas of town houses.

The delicate flowers may seem as if they are weak and in need of much care. However, don't be put off from growing them. Many species are weather-resistant, standing up to frost and snow remarkably well and requiring minimum attention. Given a top-dressing of bone-meal once a year, they will increase and produce more and more flowers all over the garden.

A free-draining soil is most important with cyclamen. Plants will tolerate an alkaline or an acid area, but not waterlogged ground. Whether you garden on clay, sand, rich humus or a peaty soil, the hardy species will flourish — even in the otherwise bare patches against fences or walls facing north-east. However, it is advisable to mix some grit and leaf mould in with the clay to make a friable compost, which will drain more easily.

It is possible to grow a collection representative of the genus in a small garden, but for best results, pay special attention to which species do better in sun and which species are more suitable for a shady site. If there is also space for a greenhouse or a frame, the more tender sorts can be kept under glass.

The following species may be grown outside in a cool climate without cover: *hederifolium, hederifolium album*, common forms of *coum, parviflorum, cilicium typicum, cilicium* var. *intaminatum* and *mirabile*. The following species are hardy, but they should be given a more sheltered place: the rare silvered forms of *coum* (especially *coum* var. *caucasicum*), *purpurascens, pseudibericum, trochopteranthum* and common forms of *repandum*.

Although it is possible to grow some of the following species

76

outside in the warmer areas of countries with a cool climate, it is generally advisable to grow them under glass: *africanum*, *balearicum*, *creticum*, *cyprium*, *graecum*, *libanoticum*, *persicum*, *repandum album*, *repandum* var. *rhodense*, *repandum* var. *peloponnese* and *rohlfsianum*.

The houseplant strains of *persicum* and the species *rohlfsianum* will definitely require artificial heat in the winter. Semi-hardy species may be raised in a bulb frame, but the tubers should not be allowed to freeze. They can be protected with extra wrappings during very cold weather.

In a Frame

It is possible to keep a representative collection of cyclamen species in the garden without heat if they are protected with a frame. Where there is plenty of space, it is better to have more than one frame: one for the species that thrive in shade and another for the species that require a south-facing position for summer ripening.

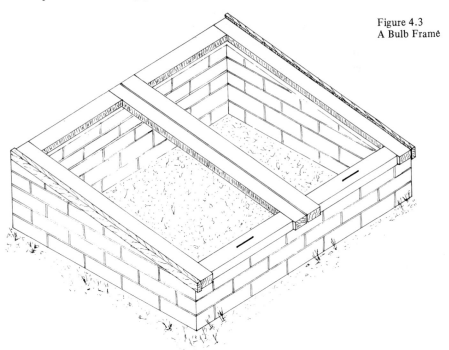

Figure 4.3
A Bulb Frame

A frame will provide protection from extreme cold, excess rain and strong winds. The glass will also stop cats and other animals from scratching up seedlings and birds from pecking off moss.

The usual method of making a general-purpose bulb frame is to place a glass or rigid plastic structure on a foundation of bricks in order to raise the roof at least 20 cm above the pots. This height allows foliage and flowers to grow without hindrance and also leaves room for newspapers or sacking to be placed on wires under the glass on very cold nights. The base of the frame is filled with sand and the pots are buried in this to just below the rims.

(All the plants discussed under the following headings can also be protected with a simple moveable frame without a base.)

In Raised Beds

Brick walls with open tops holding flower beds above paving are sometimes incorporated in modern architecture where the garden designer has made maximum use of limited space, and they are sometimes built on more than one level.

Raised beds are also found at the side of steps in older houses and country cottages. A splendid example of a bed at the top of a short wall can be seen just outside the back door of Dove Cottage, an early home of the poet Wordsworth at Grasmere in the Lake District. The patch of *hederifolium* cannot be missed by visitors as they leave the austere cottage.

In a Sink Garden

Over the last few years, there has been an increasing interest in creating miniature gardens. In the Cotswolds, some of the old sinks were carved out of solid rock, and Clarence Elliot first had the novel idea of creating gardens in cottage sinks made of limestone. He filled them with compost, rocks and rare plants, turning them into miniature alpine gardens. There are not many of the genuine stone sinks available for sale, but the glazed china kind, which have also been removed from hundreds of old houses, may be used if they are coated with a peat and concrete mixture. This weathers in time and comes to look quite like natural rock.

When making a miniature garden, it is worth taking trouble to gain an harmonious effect. The stones and plants should be placed carefully so that the finished garden resembles a natural landscape: all the rocks should slope in the same direction and be set so that the rain can run away smoothly from the surface.

Place a coil of wire-netting into the drainage hole at the base of the sink, so that rain-water can escape and not be held over-long in the soil. The compost which you choose should be rich enough to sustain the plants for many years, but be sufficiently open to allow free drainage.

The best plants for sinks or small troughs are dwarf in habit with foliage that remains tidy after flowering has finished. The stems of the flowers should be no more than 15 cm high. Hardy cyclamen fit this description better than most other plants. The most suitable species are *hederifolium*, *coum*, *cilicium*, *cilicium* var. *intaminatum*, *parviflorum* and *purpurascens*.

Many people are fascinated by the idea of having a miniature scene with a tiny coniferous tree, several large stones or tufa rocks and carpeting plants. *Frankenia*, with its minute pink flowers, variegated thyme and some of the smallest sedums and sempervivums, will spread over the soil between the stones and bulbs will grow up through the foliage.

Other plants which are good for sinks include: *Androsace sarmentosa* which forms neat umbels of flowers in April at roughly the same time as *Cyclamen pseudibericum*. Spring crocus and dwarf irises, *Dianthus*, miniature roses and silver saxifrages will also mix in well if they are kept in check and tidied at the end of every season.

A trough containing a peaty, lime-free soil will also suit cyclamen of some species, if it is well drained. Possible companion plants include dogstooth violet or *Erythronium* 'Snow-flake', *Cassiope lycopodioides*, a heather-like plant with small white bell-flowers and brown sepals, pure white snowdrops and the winter aconite *Eranthis hyemalis* or *E. cilicia* with more finely divided leaf bracts. *Cyclamen parviflorum* grows well in peaty compost in the shade and perhaps pointed or prostrate conifers and a choice gentian could be added, or mossy saxifrages. But do not put limestone chippings on this sink; otherwise, the plants which are not lime-tolerant will be lost.

Companion bulbs for a sink garden that receives sunshine for half the day include: the blue grape hyacinth (also the less common white-flowering variety), miniature daffodils and narcissus. The summer-flowering *Cyclamen purpurascens* will carry on the show of flowers when the blooms of the spring bulbs fade; autumn-flowering species continue to provide colour until late in the year, and the little *coum* brave the winter, coming into full flower immediately after Christmas.

Try to learn as much about alpine plants and their 'likes' and 'dislikes' as possible: for example, some plants will not grow where there is lime in the soil, others prefer an alkaline soil to a compost that contains mostly peat. Successful results will not be obtained by trying to grow silver saxifrages or *Dianthus* with, say gentians or *Cassiope*. In this respect, it is encouraging for the beginner to know that cyclamen tolerate lime and peat — good drainage is their main requirement. But a little care should be taken over the selection of suitable plants to grow with them.

On the Rockery

A rockery should be designed so that it merges into the surrounding garden. To be really pleasing it must look like a natural outcrop of rocks that one might find on a mountainside. Before creating a large rock garden, it is worth studying the natural harmony between rocks and plants in a mountainous region. In nature, only the tops of the rocks are exposed above soil level and pockets of scree and humus form small, isolated beds for plants. They are often protected by the over-hanging rocks from winds and driving rain. Some plants are saxatile, which means they actually root in the rocks; others such as *Androsace*, grow out from vertical cracks in the rock surface, and the tubers of some cyclamen are often found under rocks with only a long floral trunk showing against the rock face.

Limestone or sandstone are suitable rocks to choose and Westmorland stone is the favourite. This is laid down in the garden so that the rocks have the strata going in the same direction. Generally, a few large boulders create a better garden design than lots of small stones and they give a more natural effect.

Where the rockery is being built on clay, take advantage of the chance to lay a quantity of drainage material under the compost around the rocks, as most alpines thrive best on well-drained soil. The removal of all perennial weeds is another important job that must be undertaken before rock-laying and planting begins. Binder weed, couch grass and buttercups are almost impossible to weed out by hand from between precious miniature plants once they are established. Lay the drainage grit, ash, clinker, broken pots or bricks, pebbles or sand on top of the excavated site and bed the rocks into the soil so that the rock faces are deeper at the front and thinner at the back: this allows natural soil pockets to form. The whole scene should have a uniformity as if only parts of an underlayer of rock are protruding. When you come to plant, you will find that the pale cyclamen flowers stand out well against the dark rocks.

Selecting plants for the rockery is most enjoyable. There are so many rare or interesting varieties in alpine specialists' catalogues, and the London Shows of The Royal Horticulture Society make it possible to see a large range of the choice plants; it is even practicable to purchase rare treasures and order others direct. Miniature daffodils make charming companions for *Cyclamen coum*. The exquisite *Narcissus minimus* unfolds its tiny trumpets in February and is in flower with many of the snowdrops. Track down *N. cyclamineus* – the narcissus with petals reflexed like a cyclamen – and *N. juncifolius* for its dainty flowers, unusual foliage and unique fragrance. Buy *coum* to plant in separate patches of crimson, pink and white, somewhere near the star-flowers of *Chionodoxa*, glory of the snow, and the little *Iris reticulata* 'Cantab' – always a luxury.

Winter aconites are not seen in gardens as often as they should be. Arrange them with dogtooth violets (really lilies) among primroses. And a plant that is worth chancing on a rockery on accounts of its great beauty is *Cyclamen pseudibericum* – but only if you have more than one tuber, as this is a comparatively rare species and it would be a shame to lose a single specimen. It is completely hardy even in snow and can be grown outside in many areas. The crimson corolla contrasts splendidly with other spring-flowering bulbs in March.

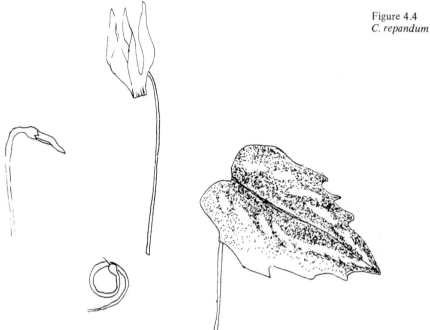

Figure 4.4
C. repandum

Cyclamen repandum will take you through late spring with primulas and auriculas. It is a woodland species that does well in a place slightly shaded by the branches of overhanging trees and the tubers should be planted deeply. Species tulips also look attractive on the rockery, but the Dutch hybrids are better kept for other parts of the garden.

Remember that most species of cyclamen rest in mid-summer and the foliage which provides such good ground cover for most of the year will almost disappear altogether. *C. purpurascens* will remain ever-green, however, and this is worth planting generously both for its ruby, fragrant flowers and for its variegated or plain leaves. This is another species that needs planting deeply for best results.

Cyclamen hederifolium will perform well every autumn no matter what the weather does. Put in the tubers and mark the places where you plant them, as they take a while to settle down and, until the foliage is growing vigorously, it might be difficult to locate them. But once established this species should increase by self-sown seed, although not so quickly as to be a nuisance – every seedling is welcome. Often flowering later in the autumn than *hederifolium*, another species to provide dainty blooms late in the year is *cilicium*, which can easily be identified by the spoon-shaped leaves and lack of auricles on the sinus. Another autumn-flowering species, *mirabile* is closely related to *cilicium* but with leaves that emerge with crimson foliage markings on the upper surface, fading as the leaves mature. This species, which is comparatively uncommon, has been seen flowering on a roadside rockery quite without protection. Do the owners of the garden know that they have such a choice plant bordering the path beside a main road? If so, their trust has been repaid, since to date the cyclamen is still there!

Figure 4.5
C. mirabile

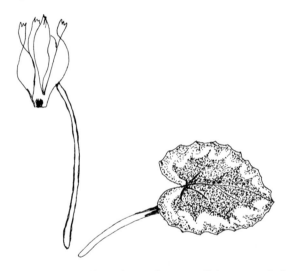

Naturalising
Cyclamen in
Large Gardens
and Light
Woodland

Cyclamen are often chosen for naturalising around churches: perhaps it is the ethereal quality of these little plants that makes them a favourite choice for planting in churchyards. Masses of the winter-flowering species *coum* grow around the church at Painswick; and the autumn-flowering species can be seen growing among headstones at Newton Ferrers, where they inspire not only the local congregation, but numerous holiday visitors from abroad. Pink and white *hederifolium* also grow in a garden along Church Path, near Ware in Hertfordshire, where they have become naturalised around the roots of a shrub and established themselves on a terrace with self-sown seeds.

Cyclamen grow semi-wild in many of the gardens belonging to the National Trust, from whom a list of gardens to be visited can be obtained (see Useful Addresses). Hidcote Manor, well described by Miss Vita Sackville-West in the 1949 journal of the Royal Horticultural Society, was the first estate to be given to the Gardens Committee. Another famous garden, Myddelton House, which was owned and described by that poetic garden writer E.A. Bowles, has *hederifolium* flowering under rare shrubs in the autumn and *coum* in bloom from Christmas to March. Both these species grow in the open at Wisley, the garden of the RHS in Surrey, where they delight many hundreds of visitors a year. However, *C. coum* is in full flower in January and *C. hederifolium* is at its best during August and September.

Many of the botanic gardens have plantings of hardy cyclamen, which have been carefully combined into the natural environment, thus bringing out the full beauty of the species. Besides the magnificent glasshouses, which must rank with the best in the world, the Royal Botanic Garden in Edinburgh has well-stocked rock and peat gardens. Hardy cyclamen have been naturalised at the Royal Botanic Gardens, Kew in the light woodland area around Cumberland Gate, where lilies, primulas and blue poppies also grow. Close by, rarer species of cyclamen can be found in the alpine house and on the rock garden.

Having seen the beauty of wide stretches of naturalised cyclamen in parks, gardeners should be encouraged to try growing them under trees and shrubs in their own gardens. Cyclamen are not difficult to establish around the roots of large trees, where the soil, lightly shaded by the leaves above, will suit them. First prepare the ground by removing perennial weeds, then rake in a little bone-meal. Plant the tubers just below the surface of the soil. It is a good idea to scatter them and dig them in where they fall, in the same manner as when planting narcissus bulbs, in order to gain an informal effect: some can be arranged in groups; some set slightly apart; and others massed together for a patch of colour.

Remember that, although it will take a few years, the tubers should steadily increase in size. Leave sufficient space between one plant and the next to allow for growth in diameter. The grass does not compete with plants under trees and the dryness rarely becomes troublesome where cyclamen are concerned. When planting under shrubs, avoid places where branches are thick with foliage near the ground, or the cyclamen may be hidden from view.

CHAPTER 5

The Species

In this chapter, I have set out under each flowering season, those species which flower during the spring, summer, autumn and winter. Each species is dealt with under the appropriate season, and Table 5.1 provides an alphabetical checklist of the various species.

Table 5.1:
Alphabetical
Checklist of
Species

Species and Forms	Flowering Season
C. africanum (17)	Autumn
C. balearicum (2)	Spring
C. cilicium (7)	Autumn
var. *intaminatum*	
C. commutatum (18)	Autumn
C. coum (4)	Winter
var. *caucasicum*	
C. creticum (3)	Spring
C. cyprium (10)	Autumn
C. graecum (14)	Autumn
C. hederifolium (16)	Autumn
C. libanoticum (9)	Spring
C. mirabile (11)	Autumn
C. parviflorum (6)	Winter
C. persicum (12)	Spring
C. pseudibericum (8)	Spring
C. purpurascens (15)	Summer
var. *colchicum*	
var. *fatrense*	
C. repandum (1)	Spring
var. *peloponnese*	
var. *rhodense*	
C. rohlfsianum (13)	Autumn
C. trochopteranthum (5)	Winter

Note: The number in parenthesis after each species refers to the reference numbers used in the distribution map on p. x, and the chromosome table on page 108.

C. purpurascens Mill

The European cyclamen, as it is commonly called (the name has only comparatively recently been changed back from *europaeum* to *purpurascens*) is evergreen, and perpetual flowering has been recorded. When not flowering continuously, it usually follows its form *fatrense* into flower, so that in early summer — mid- to late June — *C. purpurascens* var. *fatrense* is the only hardy cyclamen in bloom, but by early July two different forms of the species should be in full bloom.

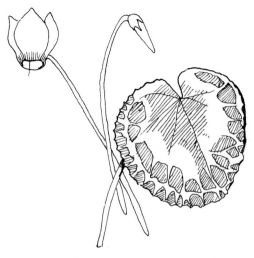

Figure 5.1
C. purpurascens

There is some friendly disagreement as to whether *purpurascens* grows better in sun or shade. In its natural habitat, it is a woodland plant thriving in the shade of a tree canopy. However, although it is one of the more common and therefore easily available species, far fewer gardeners manage to obtain fertile seed from their plants than growers of *hederifolium* or *coum*. Practical experience seems to prove that plants grown in a semi-shady place out of doors set more seed than specimens grown in a greenhouse. However, a semi-shady site can be found under a vine or climbing plant against an otherwise sunny wall.

Out of doors, *purpurascens* stay in flower until the first snows. Flowers of good forms are a deep carmine-purple, although pink forms exist and there is an extremely rare albino (see below), which unfortunately hasn't set seed readily in cultivation. All forms are strongly fragrant. The carmine and pink-flowering forms have a darker shade of the same carmine-crimson at the base of the corolla and the sinus area is wider than on other species, having the effect of making the flowers appear almost square, the petals being nearly as broad as they are long. Auricles are usually absent.

The leaves vary on different plants between round and heart-shaped: some are patterned with a lacy net of silver on dark green; others are plain matt green, and yet others have dull markings. The margins are closely denticulate.

The round and knobbly tubers produce roots all over the thick brown skin. The knobs are either the remains of floral trunks, or dormant trunks which might eventually produce new flower and leaf buds.

Always bury the tubers of this species well down in the compost and never allow them to dry out at any time in the year. Flowering-size plants can be grown from seed within three years, and tubers will grow to about 23 cm width in time. They will self-sow in some gardens.

C. purpurascens album

This form was put on display in 1944 by Mrs Saunders, and it was reported in The Alpine Garden Society Bulletin of December that year. The albino was collected by Dr Alfred de Leitner in August 1938 from Northern Croatia. Apparently, a few plants were growing near his home at Varazdin. However, a white *purpurascens* must have been in cultivation even earlier than this, as Sir Austen Chamberlain owned a white one, and he died in 1937. It is possible that the albinos in cultivation are self-sterile, in which case, seed might set after artificial cross-pollination. Only three plants are known in Europe. Mrs Saunders' daughter, Mrs Washer, still has a white-flowering plant.

C. purpurascens var. colchicum (C. colchicum Alboff)

There is some doubt over whether *colchicum* deserves species rank, or whether it is just an interesting variety of the species. It was described by Alboff in 1898; but few plants exist in cultivation. There is a specimen in the alpine house of The Munich Botanic Garden.

The flowers are similar to *purpurascens*, having the typical wide corolla mouth and short, broad petals. Prolific flowering from summer until November is possible. Professor Schwarz finds the capsules smaller than *purpurascens* var. *purpurascens*, but there are marked variations of capsule size within the species. He also reports botanical differences in leaf venation, skin of tuber, anthers, calyx lobes and seeds.

The leaves are bright green and have double dentate margins. The small heart-shaped leaves are evergreen and the layer of cells which lies just below the upper skin makes the tissue more succulent than similar tissue of other cyclamen leaves.

C. purpurascens var. *ponticum* (*C. ponticum* Pobed). This was thought to be another species, but it is a synonym of *C. purpurascens* var. *colchicum*.

C. purpurascens var. *fatrense* Halda and Sojak

Originally found in the Slovakian mountains, this cyclamen is like *purpurascens* in appearance with a similar shaped tuber. Flowers open in early June and last well into autumn. They vary from plant to plant but are usually larger and more deeply carmine-coloured than the common type found in southern Europe, and just as strongly scented.

The plain green leaves are larger and different in appearance from the plain-leaf form of *purpurascens*, although both have denticulate margins. They are evergreen and characteristically veined.

Like *purpurascens*, deep planting seems to suit the tubers of *fatrense*.

C. africanum Boiss and Reuter

Autumn Flowering

This is a handsome species with generally bolder flowers and leaves than the more readily available *hederifolium*. Under cold glass or on a kitchen windowsill the flowering period is extended right up until Christmas, which is a great advantage for the amateur gardener looking for late autumn colour.

Several forms are available. One form is so like *hederifolium* that it is difficult — but always possible — to detect the difference. *C. africanum* will not survive frost. A typical form has large leaves, which are among the largest in the genus. They are leathery in texture; pure light green, or with dull markings; other forms have a rather attractive fresh green pattern on dark green. Generally, the leaf may be heart-shaped and pointed or heart-shaped and lobed, or broadly ivy-shaped. The margins are a distinctive feature with braille-like thickening which can be clearly recognised when touched. The petioles of *hederifolium* are creeping, whereas in *africanum* they are more likely to arise perpendicularly to the tuber. Another characteristic of *africanum* is the habit of producing leaves with the flowers — in *hederifolium* it is more usual to have a flush of flowers before the leaves appear, although there is a period when foliage and flowers persist together.

Bernard Sparkes, Chairman of the Cyclamen Society, exhibited a large display of *africanum* and *hederifolium* at the November 1981 Show of the RHS at Westminster. Visitors to the Show were thus able to compare the wide range of forms and leaf shapes of both species.

The flowers, which come in all shades of pink, are produced in abundance; sometimes they are fragrant. All the corollas have auricles and the colour of the anthers is yellow, in contrast to the reddish shade of the anthers of *hederifolium*. However, this characteristic is difficult to determine with any accuracy, as many forms exist between the two distinct species.

The *africanum* tuber is corky in texture, grey-brown in colour and flat like a thick pancake in shape. It is capable of growing in size quite quickly when in a warm house, especially if planted in a suitable compost. A width of 30 cm is not common in cultivation; but a number of specialists have show-plants of this size. Flowering usually commences in the third year from sowing; occasionally in the second year.

Roots emerge all over the tuber, whereas the roots of *hederifolium* are arranged at the sides and top, but not over the oval base. However, this can be confusing since there are interspecific crosses between *africanum* and *hederifolium* which also root over the whole tuber. But true africanum has succulent and shiny leaves.

C. cilicium Boiss and Heldr. (1843)

This dainty species is often grown as semi-hardy in an alpine house. It looks very well there, but in fact it is completely hardy in most areas in Britain, growing in colonies alongside *coum* and *hederifolium*, and giving no more trouble than these two remarkably hardy species.

The flowering period extends from mid-autumn to mid-winter. The pale-pink flowers of the typical *cilicium* all have deep carmine blotches on the rather narrow sinus, which has no auricles. The corolla lobes measure 10-18 mm on the species as a whole; but 15-18 mm if the tiny variety *intaminatum* is excluded. The petal lobes are narrower than those of *hederifolium* and there is a faint scent from most forms. Altogether *C. cilicium* is fairly easy for the gardener to identify.

The leaves emerge with the flower buds. They are neatly spoon-shaped with dashes or bands of silvering around the margins, which are entirely or remotely toothed. The collectors' form, with Dr Peter Davis' number: P.D. 25889, has particularly well-silvered leaves and is often seen at Alpine Garden Society competitions.

The tubers of *cilicium* are small, smooth-skinned and round in shape. They are quickly separated from a batch of *hederifolium* tubers, as the new foliage emerges from the centre of the top, and the roots grow from a central ring at the base.

Flowering plants can be raised from seed within two years; but plants become more floriferous in succeeding years.

C. cilicium var. *intaminatum* Meikle, RBG, Edinb. (1978)

This is the smallest known cyclamen. It was referred to until recently as *C. cilicium var.* or *C. alpinum* and a fine form first collected from the wild in 1934 was labelled E.K. Balls 669a.

The flowers are the most distinguishing feature, although specialists have no difficulty in identifying plants by their leaves. The corolla is white tinged pink or white with no auricles and no crimson sinus. Fine transparent veins running up the corolla lobes have the effect of making the sinus appear grey, and for this reason *intaminatum* is sometimes called the 'grey-nose' species. The flowers are small compared to other cyclamen: corolla lobes measure only 10-15 mm and there is no fragrance.

Figure 5.2
C. cilicium var.
intaminatum

X ½

The various forms have been given numbers in the past, for example there is the variegated 669a and the plain-leaf 628. However, the varietal epithet covers all known forms at present. It is interesting to note the recognisable foliage and flower combinations; perhaps cultivar names will follow in the future:

1. white flowers; plain foliage;
2. white flowers; wide silver margin on foliage;
3. pink flowers; plain foliage;
4. pink flowers; wide silver margin on foliage.

There is also a pattern similar to the 669a plant illustrated in Mrs Saunders' booklet. This has pale pink flowers and leaves with silver markings that resemble the holes made by nails in a horseshoe. However, results of experiments conducted here seem to suggest that forms with the dot-like silver pattern and forms with the wide silver margin will interbreed and produce mixed progeny including plain-leaf offspring. This might be because the silver-foliage parent was heterozygous for leaf-colour, since the plain-leaf forms appear to breed true, i.e. no silver-leaf forms have been amongst the seedlings of an isolated plain-leaf plant.

The leaves are easily distinguished from *cilicium* var. *cilicium*, being round to kidney-shaped rather than spoon-shaped, and there is an overall daintiness due to the miniature size of flowers and leaves. Most tubers in cultivation are small, measuring about 3 cm at first flowering about two to three years after sowing. However, tubers which have been kept for a number of years do grow larger, eventually reaching about 18 cm in width; but the leaves and flowers remain miniature.

C. commutatum Schwarz and Lepper

A species found in north-west Africa, but distinguishable from *africanum* (also of Algeria) only by a chromosome count. A cross

89

with *hederifolium* (34 chromosomes) resulted in sterile offspring — probably because of the different chromosome number. *C. commutatum* (68 chromosomes) can be considered as a separate species for this reason. The growing habits of both *commutatum* and *africanum* are not the same as *hederifolium*. The flowering season of *commutatum* is extended right until Christmas. Although *commutatum* x *hederifolium* crosses are not successful, *africanum* x *hederifolium* crosses are thought possible as plants displaying intermediate forms have been bred, i.e. plants having some of the characteristics of both species. However, the interspecific crosses can be distinguished from the pure-bred *africanum* and the pure-bred *hederifolium*. The separation of *commutatum* and *africanum* can be only of interest to botanists, since horticulturalists will continue to call all plants with large thick leaves and flowers with straight stems *africanum*, especially if they are not hardy.

C. cyprium Kotschy

This species only grows wild on the island of Cyprus. The best plants are often exchanged amongst collectors, although some good forms are sold by specialist nurserymen.

The strongly fragrant flowers are sometimes pale pink when they first unfold, quickly turning to white as they mature. Corolla lobes are very daintily narrow at the mouth and marked with a unique pink pattern round the sinus. The auricles are prominent and the petals long and twisted. Plants are usually in full bloom in late autumn, lasting up to Christmas if protected from the cold; but losing both flowers and foliage if exposed to frost.

The foliage on good specimens can be brightly coloured in olive, yellow and stone, as well as dark and light green; others have vivid patches of silvery-white on a dark green background. Less well-marked specimens have mottled olive-green and dark green on the upper surface; yet others are olive-green with silver markings, or no markings. The lower surface of the leaf is usually beetroot red. The broad, pointed leaves often persist throughout winter under glass without heating, but the species is not generally considered suitable for growing outside without glass protection in cold climates, although Lewis Palmer grew this species outside in Winchester.

The tuber is sometimes slow to come back into growth after the summer resting season, especially if June and July are cool. There is often a flattened disc-like platform at the top, where the new leaf and flower buds arise and the roots emerge acentrally from the base. The shape is round and the skin is browny-grey. Tubers can flower when they measure only 2.5 cm, and they reach this size about three years from flowering.

C. graecum Link 1835

A beautiful species, but more difficult to bring into flower in a cool climate than *hederifolium*, although plants have been known to flower outside in sheltered districts.

The flowers appear every autumn under glass if the resting tubers are correctly watered during the summer. It has been discovered recently, that if plants are not dried off completely during June and July, but allowed some moisture at root level, better results are gained. In their natural habitat, the tubers are often found under rocks, where the fleshy roots reach right down to water levels below the hot, dry surface soil. Bedding pots in grit or sand has been found helpful, although the problem then is that the roots work their way through the hole in the base of the pot.

The flowers which bear auricles vary in colour from almost white with a carmine sinus, through the palest pinks, to a deep carmine-red which has the sinus crimson colour running up the lobes of the corolla in two or three streaks. The petals can be straight or elegantly twisted, long and narrow or widely curved; most are large in size with violet anthers rather than the reddish-brown of *hederifolium*, and there is a pink protruding stigma. The fruiting pedicel coils from the middle or a point close to the tuber rather than from the capsule downwards as in most other species.

Leaf buds appear with the flower buds or a little after them. The mostly heart-shaped leaves are closely denticulate and the velvety texture is much appreciated by cyclamen specialists who collect leaf forms for their brilliant white marbling or silver bands and blotches; some leaves are pale green without any silvering, and others are an unusual grey-green with intricate lacy patterns like snowflakes.

The globose tuber is more oval in shape than the other species with a rough, corky skin and thick, fleshy roots. It produces long floral trunks which measure 60 cm or more in the wild. In cultivation, the tuber can grow to about 20 cm in diameter. Plants flower for the first time three to four years after sowing.

C. graecum was originally described from specimens collected by F. Berger from the Peloponnese in the early nineteenth century, and for the first forty years after the discovery, the naming of the species was confused. When studying cyclamen in 1906, Hildebrand noticed that the pedicels coil from the base upwards, rather than from the capsule downwards, as in most other species, and this helped with identification. The Cyprus forms have been given the name of *cyprograecum* but this is not a separate species; they are reputedly more difficult to flower than Greek forms in cultivation.

Table 5.2: Synonyms for *C. graecum*		
C. aegineticum	Not in use, except in botanical history
C. gaidurowrysii	The word *gaidurowrysii* is sometimes used to describe a geographical form of *C. graecum*, but it is not acceptable as a species epithet
C. Gaydurowrysii (Glasau)	Not in use, except in botanical history
C. hederifolium	A wrongly applied synonym
C. maritimum	No longer accepted
C. miliarakesii	No longer accepted
C. mindleri	A geographical variation. Not in use, except in botanical history.
C. pentelici	A non-acceptable synonym
C. pseudograecum	A non-acceptable synonym
C. pseudomaritimum	A non-acceptable synonym

C. graecum album

The discovery of a pure white-flowering form is described in the Cyclamen Society's *Journal* by Mrs Erna Frank, who went with her husband and Manfred Koenen of the Botanical Gardens in Bonn, to the Peloponnese in 1980, and saw 'tens of thousands' of pink-flowering *graecum*. It is easy to understand their excitement when they came across two plants with absolutely white flowers. When they found the plants, the botanist nearly fainted with joy.

C. hederifolium Aiton. (*C. neapolitanum* Ten.)

This species probably gains its popularity on account of its hardiness – it is possible to brush frost off plants in pots growing out of doors and take them to shows. Buds usually appear at the end of summer, about the beginning of August, and flowering continues until the end of autumn. Some of the interspecific crosses with *africanum* keep flowering until Christmas. One strain of *hederifolium* will come into flower early and another late, so that the flowering period is prolonged for many months – a good reason for collecting several strains of one species.

The flower colour is pale rose with a carmine sinus, although a wide range of rose tints and shades can be found. The corolla lobes vary in length from plant to plant, but the average is about 2 cm. Many blooms grow on one plant – more appearing each year as the size of the tuber increases; fifty flowers on one plant is not uncommon. There is a scented form which is delightful, but comparatively rare and consequently difficult to obtain. It also seems to be slightly more tender, which probably accounts for the rarity. It is far more difficult to track down than the white-flowering form, which was quite rare at one time, and is still less common than the pink. The anthers are brownish-red and the stigma does not protrude. There are auricles at the mouth of the corolla.

Foliage is as spectacular as on some of the rarer and more exotic species. The leaves usually emerge after the flowers and they vary tremendously in pattern and shape, which adds to the interest for cyclamen enthusiasts. It has been said many times that no two are alike, and this seems to be true. There are patterns ranging from the all-green leaf — not common — to the heavily silvered leaf: some forms are light yellow-green or light apple green in the centre with a dark almost black-green border; others are dark in the centre with a light green margin. In between are plants with leaves marked in all manner of intricate lacy designs. Perhaps the most striking is the strain known as 'Bowles Apollo'. The foliage of a good form of this is marked with dark and light greens in vivid contrast like a patchwork quilt. A splendid specimen was exhibited at the first Cyclamen Society Conference at Wye College. There is also variety in the shapes of the leaves, which can be tiny, heart-shaped, large heart-shaped; long, narrow, dagger or spearhead-shaped; or angular ivy-shaped. The margins are toothed, although not usually as coarsely and heavily toothed as on *africanum*. The leaves, which may be pointed or rounded at the tip, remain on the plant for most of the year. Many lose their foliage during mid-summer for the whole of June and July. However, young plants and seedlings should be encouraged to keep their leaves right through the resting season. This involves careful attention to the amount of shade and rainwater (or tap water) each plant receives.

The tubers which root from the top and sides are flat and corky. They can be induced to flower in their second season when grown in suitable surroundings; but more often they flower in the third year, when about 6 cm in width. They get larger every year until they reach the size of a large plate or the top of a small coffee-table, living longer than most other garden plants: specimens over 150 years old have been recorded. (Tubers measuring 36 cm across are to be seen growing on the Isle of Man. (C.S.Jour.III.2.))

C. hederifolium album

There are many white-flowering forms of the species, but as there is considerable variation in flower size and foliage pattern from plant to plant, the name 'album' does not stand for cultivar status, in which there should be uniformity in flower and foliage, so that two specimens show no more differences between them than identical twins. However, it seems more than likely that good forms will be isolated in cultivation and eventually pure breeding varieties should be given cultivar names. The seed nurseries are beginning to take an interest in the hardy species, and as *hederifolium* seed is the most readily available, it is possible that a wider range of varieties within the species will be listed in catalogues before long.

C. mirabile Hildebr. (1906)

Although given separate status this species comes under the general umbrella of *cilicium*, as they are closely related. It is fascinating to realise that as recently as 1950, *mirabile* was almost unknown. One plant had been examined and described by a botanist at the turn of the century, but Doorenbos, when studying the genus later, was obliged to write: 'As it has never been found since, we will not copy Hildebrand's description.' Luckily, in 1956, Dr Peter Davis and Dr Polunin discovered another plant; and in 1965 further supplies were found. Now there are quite a number of plants of this species on the market. During the last fifteen years, cyclamen specialists have purchased tubers from chain stores believing them to be other species while in the dry state. When they began to grow, they were obviously *mirabile* wrongly labelled. Quite a pleasant surprise, since *mirabile* is still a rarer plant than *cilicium*.

The pink flowers are much the same in appearance as *cilicium*, except that the edges of the corolla lobes are finely toothed at the tips. There are no auricles and the petals are narrow and twisted with a dark blotch at the mouth of the corolla; the inner surface is covered with small gland cells. The flowering period continues from late summer until November.

Leaves of the best forms are easy to distinguish from *cilicium* leaves, or leaves of any other cyclamen. There is a bright crimson tint on the upper surface of the young lamina. Sometimes this is in a hastate pattern which is clearly defined and sometimes it is a paler tint across the central zone. Try not to judge this until you have seen a number of plants, as the brightness of the tint varies considerably. Some leaves have the red colour merging with the silver. Apparently Hildebrand gave the plant the name *mirabile* on account of this red coloration. At least it lets us have some idea of his feeling of joy when he saw this very different type of leaf for the first time: on looking at a newly opened young leaf and finding it red inside instead of the usual green, it is possible to catch for a second his excitement. In shape, the leaves are generally more toothed than *cilicium* leaves and the petioles tend to be straight rather than slanting at an angle away from the centre of the tuber, as in *cilicium*.

The tubers are usually larger and more corky than *cilicium* var. *cilicium* and the roots develop from a ring around the base instead of from the centre of the base; and they are thickly fibrous rather than thinly fibrous. Flowering occurs during the third season after sowing when tubers are about 4 cm in width. Plants here proved to be as hardy if not hardier than *cilicium* during the snow and frost of December 1981. Leaves didn't curl as *cilicium* leaves did.

C. rohlfsianum Aschers

The rarest of the autumn-flowering species, *rohlfsianum* is difficult to find and expensive to buy. It is not hardy and needs some warmth during the winter in cold climates. The species, first collected by Rohlfs in 1879, was described in 1897.

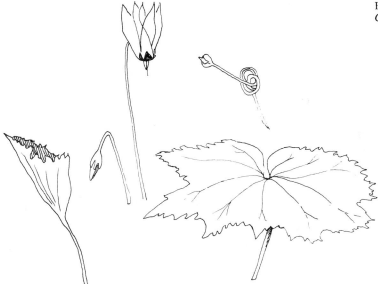

Figure 5.3
C. rohlfsianum

The fragrant flowers are deep pink and worth waiting for, as they are different from other cyclamen. The anthers are uniquely arranged, forming a cone that projects beyond the mouth of the corolla. This characteristic is also interesting to botanists as it indicates that the genus *Cyclamen* and the genus *Dodecatheon* have common ancestors, since the latter displays a similar botanical feature. Otherwise, the flowers are long and pointed with twisted lanceolate corolla lobes. The sinus has deeply coloured crimson triangular patches pointing upwards from the mouth of the auriculate corolla. The flowers appear with the foliage in September and continue until about the end of November, and the fruiting pedicel coils from base to tip, unlike most other cyclamen.

The leaves emerge before the flowers from any point at the top of the tuber and they are often widely spaced. The young leaves are carried on pink petioles covered in browny-pink hairs; but when fully developed, they lose the hairs and have a wavy appearance, the lamina becoming broad with large lobes and dentate margins. Some forms have silvered leaves; others plain, and the colour can be light or dark green with a matt or shining upper surface and green or red reverse. There is a half-moon shape were petiole meets leaf: this is evident even on the seedling, although the baby leaf is entire — the lobes forming on large mature leaves, which can grow as large as an outstretched hand.

The tuber is uneven in shape as though someone has taken odd bites out of it, eventually growing big and corky, becoming flattened on the top, forming a wide plateau as much as 20 cm or more across. The hairy, brown roots usually emerge from the sides.

Winter
Flowering

C. coum Mill. (1768)

As can be seen from Table 5.3, more confusion has arisen over the naming of plants within the *coum* group, than other cyclamen in the genus; but the *coum* epithet now covers the many forms within the species.

Fred Buglass wrote on this species in a recent Cyclamen Society *Journal*: 'I produced the widest variety of colour, flower size and leaf form that could be imagined. Pale green leaves with dark green and silver green patterns, dark green dull surface, dark green polished surface, round in shape, flattened heart shape with underside varying from deep crimson to almost dull green. I fell in love with this species for its variety.'

The Director of The Royal Horticultural Gardens, C.D. Brickell, also writing in a Cyclamen Society *Journal* divides the group into two: *C. coum* var. *coum* and *C. coum* var. *caucasicum*. He states that: 'Out of the morass of names we are basically left with two definable entities in the *C. coum* group.'

It seems that the species will produce hybrids with closely related forms within the *coum* group. However, some of the recognisable forms with distinctive foliage markings and colours will breed true if isolated, bringing forth generations of identical offspring. As increased interest in the genus continues to lead to more knowledge, cultivar names will follow, although at present it is impossible to say how long it will be before true breeding strains are registered.

One of the advantages of this extremely hardy species is that it bravely puts up its flowers in mid-winter. Flower buds appear in December and continue to open until March. The corolla is short and wide and the flowers have often been described as dumpy — a word that does not give a clear idea of their beauty! *C. coum* flowers provide a curious contrast of natural forms, when compared with the autumn-flowering species, since the petals are not long and twisted; they are interesting with their compact dwarf shapes.

Table 5.3: Synonyms for *C. coum*

C. abchasicum	Not in use, except in botanical history
C. adzharicum	Not acceptable, other than in the history of the genus
C. coum album	White-flowering form of *coum* var. *coum*
C. atkinsii	Formerly thought to be a hybrid between *coum* and *persicum*
C. atkinsii roseum	A common, but not acceptable, name for the pink-flowering forms of *coum* var. *coum*
C. coum ssp. *caucasicum* Schwarz	Synonym for *C. coum* var. *caucasicum*
C. coum var. *caucasicum* Meikle	
C. coum var. *coum* Mill	
C. hiemale	No longer accepted as a separate species
C. hymale	Synonym for *coum* var. *coum* (as above)
C. coum ibericum	Synonym for *C. coum* var. *caucasicum*; not acceptable
C. kusnetzovic	Synonym for forms of *coum* found in the Crimea
C. coum Macka	Geographical variation of *C. coum* var. *coum* (white 'eye') – not a cultivar; i.e. it is also possible to find plants of *C. coum* var. *caucasicum* (pink 'eye') in the same area, as there is an overlap of the varieties of *coum* in the region
C. orbiculatum	Not in use, except in botanical history
C. coum Tirebolu	Geographical variation; not a cultivar
C. coum Urfa	Geographical variation; not a cultivar
C. vernale	Wrongly applied synonym for *coum* var. *coum*
C. vernum	Out-of-date synonym for *coum* var. *caucasicum*
C. vernum var. *caucasicum*	Unacceptable synonym for *C. coum* var. *caucasicum*

Flower colours are pale rose-pink, pale and dark magenta, crimson and white. All forms of *coum* var. *coum* have dark blotches at the base of the petals with a white area at the mouth of the corolla. The white patches are missing on *trochopteranthum* and *parviflorum*, and they are pale pink or purple on *coum* var. *caucasicum*. The white or light coloured area is sometimes known as the 'eye'. There are no auricles and the anthers are yellow. The stigma does not project beyond the corolla.

The leaves are commonly dark green and kidney-shaped with a dull or shiny surface, but there are various forms with light green hastate pattern markings. Collectors look for plants with wide bands of silver round the margins. These have been bred from E.K. Balls 371 or the so-called 'Nymans' variety. There is also a rare form with leaves entirely covered with silver E.K. Balls 771. Further tests are needed to discover if 371 and 771 will breed true when isolated. It seems likely that they will, since both these forms can be identified quite easily by gardeners and a number of identical plants exist. Other forms have been given names, which are no longer accepted: *hiemale* was supposed to be particularly early flowering, and it is always among the first to bloom every year here; *atkinsii* was a special shade of pink, and M&T 4051 a deep ruby-red. Even though they are all called just *Cyclamen coum* now, specialists will continue to pick out the plants with the best leaves and the most beautiful flowers.

The tuber is round with a thin smooth skin and there is an indentation at the top where the new foliage and flowers develop. Roots spring from the centre of the base. Plants can reach a flowering size of 3 cm in their third year. They grow less quickly than *hederifolium*, but floral trunks are often present on older tubers.

C. coum var. caucasicum (C. caucasicum Schwarz)

There is still a need for further research and classification within the *coum* group. At present, it can be said that there are recognisable, but as yet unnamed, forms of cyclamen found in and around the Caucasus: some have flowers and leaves that are twice the size of the ordinary *coum*. The leaves are a different shape; and to those who have only seen the common forms of *coum* var. *coum*, quite un-*coum*-like. They are heart-shaped and shallowly toothed with silver markings. Good specimens are much sort after by cyclamen enthusiasts. The bold flowers have pointed corolla lobes and a pale, purple-pink eye instead of the *coum* white eye.

This variety has also been described as *abchasicum*, *adzharicum*, *circassicum*, *elegans*, *ibericum* and *vernum* by botanists and horticulturalists in the past.

C. parviflorum Pobed. (1946)

The smallest of the *coum* type of cyclamen is difficult to obtain as it is rare in cultivation, but it is well worth seeking out. It was collected from Turkey in 1914 and has been available to gardeners since about 1960. This really is the dwarf of the genus.

The flowers are an unusual shade of lavender-pink and they do not have the white area on the basal blotch of carmine colour. The petals unfold from late winter to spring, but the buds appear as early as late autumn and hold over winter flat against the top of the tuber. The short pedicels carry the flowers just above foliage level, each corolla measuring about 5-10 mm in length.

Suborbicular-shaped dark green leaves are tiny with entire margins. They are almost evergreen, staying on the plant for most of the year. The seed-leaves — one cotyledon per seedling — are a lighter green and more pointed than the true leaves. This makes it easy to pick out first-year seedlings from second-year seedlings at a glance.

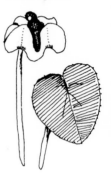

Figure 5.4
C. parviflorum,
Dwarf Species

Tubers are small, bright bead-green, thin skinned and round in shape. There is a central growing point on top and a central root-ring at the base, which continues in growth all the year. Flower buds develop for the first time on three-year-old tubers, some as small as 2 cm in width. Some doubt has been expressed as to this species' hardiness — a tray of seedlings came through the winter in the open here in Essex with only a sheet of glass as protection, and tubers which were growing in a cold frame came through the frost of winter 1981 without losing their leaves. Snow was piled high on top of the frame and no extra covers were placed over the plants beneath the lights. Losses are more likely to occur during the hot, dry days of summer, when there is a danger that plants will not get enough water. Tubers seem to stand extreme cold better than lack of moisture at the roots. They are more susceptible to dryness than other cyclamen.

C. trochopteranthum Schwarz (1975) (*C. alpinum* Sprenger (1892))

Until recently, this species was known as *C. alpinum* by botanists, gardeners and nurserymen. It is similar to *coum*, except that the corolla lobes never become fully reflexed, but always remain at an angle of 90°, looking like a child's painting of a windmill, or an aeroplane propeller.

Each flower is about 4 cm wide and there are light pink as well as dark pink forms, although the deeper shade is more popular. The ruby blooms have a dark mouth to the corolla but no white area and the base of the blotch is straight rather than three-pronged like *coum*.

The leaves can be distinguished from *coum* leaves by the specialist, as *trochopteranthum* has foliage more like *cilicium* with splashes of colour around a hastate pattern and a very shiny upper surface which is usually red on the reverse. The truncate-oval shape is quite different from the kidney-shape of *coum* var. *coum*.

99

The tuber is similar in shape to *coum* and plants are hardy, although protection from excess rain is advisable. The leaves turn dull in cold weather, losing their turgidity as soon as the temperature drops. The flowering period is from winter into spring, and plants begin to form buds late in the third year from sowing; although hardy, they are best kept in a cold frame or alpine house.

Spring Flowering

C. balearicum Willk.

The flowers unfold their wavy, pointed petals in March and April. They are usually white and fragrant, although occasionally pink forms are found. When grown in a cool house or an alpine house, the flower stems remain short, holding the flower heads just above the foliage.

Plants are valued for their leaves as much as for their flowers. The largish leaves are thin, ovate or cordate in shape, with well-marked splashes of silver on a bluish-grey upper surface; red below. They are slightly denticulate.

The tubers are small and flat, rooting from the centre of the base. They need protection from frost and the leaves must be shielded from scorching sun. Seed sown in late summer without heat germinates in late autumn.

C. balearicum x repandum. Graham Simpson, Treasurer of the Cyclamen Society, reports having grown seed resulting from a cross between these two species. Seven seeds germinated; three had crimson flowers and resembled the *repandum* parent; two took after the *balearicum* parent, and two had pink flowers.

C. creticum Hildebr.

This woodland species grows in silt in the shade in deep gullies and cracks in rocks. Quantities can be found on Crete and plants were collected and brought home by alpine gardeners before the conservation laws were strengthened. Plants are still comparatively rare, probably because they are tender and not easy to bring through the winter in cold climates. They need protection from frost, although specimens have been grown outside in very sheltered areas under shrubs.

White flowers unfold from March until May perfuming the alpine house with a faint fragrance, more noticeable if a number of plants are grown. There is no carmine sinus and auricles are absent. The dainty petals are narrow and ribbon-like; they have been compared to the very rare albino *repandum*.

Obcordate-shaped leaves are small and pointed. They are dark green spotted or splashed with silver on the upper surface and deep red below — similar to the Peloponnese form of *repandum*.

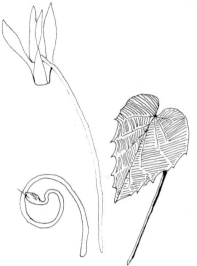

Figure 5.5
C. creticum

The tuber, which is shaped like a flattened sphere, bears roots from the centre of the base and has a thin brown skin.

C. libanoticum Hildebr.

This rare species was discovered in 1895. The original plant named by Hildebrand was found north-east of Beirut in a shady position on the slopes of mountains between rocks and tree roots, where it was locally fairly widespread. However, for a while it was thought to be extinct, until rediscovered in 1961. It is still difficult to obtain, but available from specialist nurserymen.

The fragrant flowers open pale pink in February or March from buds that form before the winter snows, but remain undeveloped until the spring. The sharply pointed, ovate petals are larger than the corolla lobes of most cyclamen: flowers measure 2.5 cm on erect 15 cm stems; and as they develop they change from pale pink to a deep, clear pink of a shade which is unique in the genus. The sinus is blotched with dark crimson bat-shaped markings.

The roundish or obcordate leaves appear at the beginning of winter, folded in half. Some forms resemble the foliage of *cyprium* in shape and pattern; but the specialist will be able to distinguish *libanoticum* by the flowering time, the individual flowers and the wide band of olive grey-green around the margins of the leaves (although occasionally the leaves are plain, dark green). They are bright red on the lower surface.

The species can be grown out of doors in dry, sunny places; but because of the rather small tubers, it is usually considered best to

101

plant in groups in pans. The tuber takes a long time to increase in size in cultivation. It is covered with groups of hairs when young, but becomes corky as it ages. The roots emerge slightly to the side of the base. Seedlings can be raised in the home quite easily.

C. persicum Mill. (1768)

All the hybrids, cultivated strains and varieties have been bred from the wild species found in the eastern Mediterranean.

When grown hardy or almost hardy in an alpine house, the foliage remains compact and bright green. Flower buds form during the summer and autumn; they develop very slowly through the winter to open in March, and the plants continue flowering until May. But if grown cold during the autumn with gentle heat at night from October onwards, the flowers open in time for Christmas. The flower colours of the species are white, pale pinks, mauves and lilacs; each with a deeply blotched purple-carmine sinus. (Vivid scarlets, deep purple-blacks and dark reds are not found in the wild.)

The blooms are held high above the foliage on long pedicels, which do not coil, but bend and become stiffly arched when the capsules are ripening. The petals are long, narrow and twisting; and the cells of the corolla carry a strong fragrance. There are no auricles.

The leaves are circular or heart-shaped, beautifully marbled or silvered, and on many forms heavily toothed: sometimes there is a dark central zone with a contrasting light margin; and sometimes the centre is light with a dark green border. Many plants have a conspicuous hastate pattern and occasionally this takes the form of a broken line resembling silver dots. Some of the leaves of this species are among the largest in the genus; others are small and neat. The foliage does not stand up to frost, therefore plants are rarely grown out of doors in Britain and countries with cool climates.

Tubers are flat and thick, and can live for a hundred years or more. Floral trunks producing pedicels and petioles are often present on older specimens. Roots emerge from the sides and the root-ring at the base; each root can be as thick as a piece of string and a floral trunk can be surrounded by these string-like roots so that they sometimes appear to have become rooted offsets, when in fact the roots belong to the parent tuber.

C. persicum album. A white-flowering natural form of the species was given the name *C. aleppicum ssp. puniceum* by Fisch; but this is not considered as a separate species today. The name is recorded as an historical synonym for *C. persicum.* (I. de Haan and J. Doorenbos, 1951).

C. pseudibericum Hildebr.

A plant was sent to Hildebrand in 1901 from the well-known bulb firm of van Tubergen, but a Turkish botanist was the first to discover this species, which many gardeners consider one of the most attractive in the genus.

Flowers of choice forms are a bright red-pink, a different colour from other spring-flowering cyclamen, and much larger and bolder than *coum*. At the base of the corolla lobes there is a spectacular pair of white patches surrounded by a deep brown-purple area, and there are no auricles. They grow well in the shade, but tolerate a fair amount of sun in a greenhouse. The flowering time is usually March, but some plants come into bloom in February under cold glass, where the colour of the petals and the fragrance is most welcome so early in the year. The buds emerge in autumn, but do not develop until the first light days of spring.

The cordate leaves are often brilliantly marbled and they remain decorative throughout the winter. They are surprisingly hardy remaining turgid even after snow falls. Lewis Palmer reported that his plants survived outside under a tree in Winchester, even in the very cold winter of 1961-62, and here in Essex, the foliage looked undamaged after the frost and snow before Christmas 1981.

Tubers are globular-shaped and often flat at the top. The skin is corky in texture and the roots emerge from the base.

The form with red-pink, or magenta-coloured, flowers was collected by Dr Polunin on Düldül Dag, near Haruniye and distributed under Dr Peter Davis' number 26117. It was found growing with *Helleborus vesicarius* under beech trees.

There is also a rare paler pink form, which was discovered in Dörtyol, Turkey. It can occasionally be traced under the collector's number A.C. & W. 664.

C. repandum Sibth and Smith

This species was first recorded in 1806. It is a woodland plant that grows fairly freely around the Mediterranean and naturalises quite well in cultivation.

The flowers, a deep self-pink with carmine sinus, open at the end of March and last well into May. (There is a very rare albino form that does not have the red sinus.) No auricles are present and the stigma protrudes beyond the corolla mouth.

The heart-shaped leaf is toothed, lobed and pointed, and on most plants the hastate pattern is conspicuous against a light to dark green background colour. The foliage develops many months before the flowers.

The small, flattened-globular tubers have a brown skin and root from the base.

Figure 5.6
C. repandum var.
peloponnese

C. repandum album. The white-flowering form mentioned above, which is not hardy.

C. repandum var. *peloponnese*. The leaves of this form are among the most attractive in the entire genus. They are a very dark green with strongly contrasting silver or grey spots; remotely toothed, occasionally subentire. It is comparatively rare in cultivation.

C. repandum var. *rhodense* Meikle. This beautiful plant with a white corolla and crimson sinus markings is found on Rhodes. The sweetly scented blooms with long wavy petals are among the last cyclamen flowers to appear in spring. The shallowly lobed heart-shaped leaf is bright green covered with speckles of light grey.

In reply to a recent questionnaire circulated by the Cyclamen Society, only three per cent of members reported that they were growing this form which can be grown out of doors, although it is usually kept in a pot in cultivation because of its rarity. Living room shade is tolerated.

CHAPTER 6

New Strains and Cultivars

The origin of the genus is complicated, and there is evidence that in all the important characteristics it existed at the beginning of the Tertiary geological period about sixty million years ago. Therefore, it is possible that an early form of cyclamen survived prehistoric times. Further, there is evidence (but no final proof) that one original species, which was widespread, began to develop different forms when separated by shifting land surfaces.

Links with an earlier species — a common ancestor — are suggested by the genus' habit of producing adventitious roots as a last resort, as seen in *C. rohlfsianum* when in unhospitable surroundings. And again in the similarity between the better forms of *C. coum* var. *caucasicum* and *C. persicum* regarding leaf colour, shape and markings, which also suggest derivation from some perhaps now extinct common ancestor. Adaptations to regional climates are more likely to have occurred comparatively recently. But it is amazing how many of the ancient characteristics have been preserved, and there must be a reason why the species have been slow to change over countless years. Isolated regions of woodland have provided natural conservation areas in Europe and the borders of the Alps; but the possible phenomenon of apomictic production of seed, i.e. reproduction without fertilisation, might account for the many crosses that give rise to offspring which are identical to the mother plant. It has also been thought possible that fertilisation does take place, but that processes after fertilisation prevent the male-cell characteristics from being inherited.

In the Cyclamen Society *Journal*, Alisdair Aird, Show Secretary, describes a collection of choice plants exhibited on the Cyclamen Society stand at one of the RHS Shows in London: '*C. graecum* included a group of Fred Buglass's rare and attractive island forms', adding that: 'An interesting point with these was the apparent stability of the genetic material.' The seedlings of various ages were all showing the same leaf pattern as the mother plant.

If cyclamen have all evolved from one original type, that early plant could have resembled *repandum* — a species which is fairly widespread. And it is thought that the rare form of *purpurascens*, known as *colchicum*, might be an isolated surviving ancestor of *hederifolium*, which could have been the ancestor of *africanum*. It is interesting that although many cyclamen species are alike to look at (i.e. in their morphological characteristics) they are intersterile. It is also interesting that species with similar chromosome numbers are not necessarily found together in one geographical or ecological area. There is an overlap of species that grow naturally in several regions around the Mediterranean.

Figure 6.1
C. hederifolium

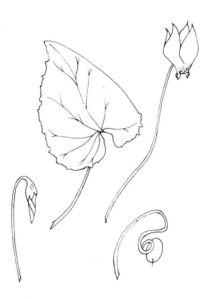

The genus *Cyclamen* is grouped into species according to appearance, or morphological characteristics and whether plants will interbreed. With the discovery of genetics, selective breeding can now take place. Plant breeders study the offspring that appear in successive generations from just one pair of plants and, taking the laws of genetics into account, can predict the size and shape of plants, and the possibility of producing a particular colour.

The First Cultivated Strains of Cyclamen persicum

In the *persicum* species, modern cultivars have all been bred from a few mutations of the wild species. The species came from Cyprus, and was cultivated in the Chelsea Physic Garden and recorded at Kew Garden in 1731. 'Rubrum Grandiflorum' appeared in 1867, followed by 'Giganteum' in 1870, and interest was transferred from

106

large flowers to giant flowers. Once the increase in size of the showy blooms had been obtained, nurserymen turned their attention to separating the pinks from the bluey-mauves, and when a salmon-pink flower had been bred, after careful crossing and back-crossing, the salmon-scarlet began to emerge. More recently, the vivid scarlet has been produced.

In 1882-3 James Carter, Dunnett and Beale, Seed Farmers and Merchants, included a number of varieties of cyclamen in their 'Vegetable and Floral Novelties' list. They were reputed to be the finest colours available and were awarded First Class Certificates of Merit by The Royal Horticultural Society and The Royal Botanic Society. The names of the varieties were 'White Swan', 'Duke of Connaught', 'Rosy Morn', 'Picturatum', 'Giganteum Compactum Magnificum' and 'Giganteum Roseum Compactum'. The giant salmon was sold by Suttons in 1894 as 'Salmon Queen'. One of the earliest florists' forms of *persicum* to have the pot-plant shape was the popular variety 'Rosa von Zehlendorf'. Splendid giant hybrids bred by Stoldt were illustrated in 1902. In 1916, Maarse of Aalsmeer introduced 'Carmine-Salmon', and a little over ten years later, Braukmann produced a new variety 'Flamingo' which was dark salmon with a light margin. In 1948 the successful variety 'Apple Blossom' appeared.

Each hereditable characteristic is controlled by two genes, one on each of a pair of chromosomes, found in the male and female reproductive cells. These genes control a wide range of characteristics — corolla colour, shape of lobe, length of stem, etc. — and they are arranged on the chromosomes like beads on a necklace. One gene from each male and female cell passes into the offspring. If a plant breeds true for, say, flower colour, it is possibly *homozygous* for flower colour, i.e. the genes from both parents are identical. Plants carrying two different genes for the same characteristic are said to be *heterozygous*.

One of the main reasons for the research on the genus *Cyclamen* which Professor Wellensiek began in the Netherlands during 1946, was to see if crosses would be successful between any of the other species and the cultivated forms of *persicum* in order to help breeders raise new varieties. Breeding plants became rather difficult through the war, but by 1957 Germany was able to produce a list of 119 varieties of *persicum* for the project in Holland.

In 1962, a paper was published describing early work on an International Name List of *Cyclamen* cultivars. Professor Wellensiek and his colleagues worked on aspects such as status, breeding history and morphological characteristics of the cultivars, as well as the

Raising New Varieties — A Look at Genetics

study of chromosomes, the examination of the flower colours and the genetics of the genus.

Table 6.1: Chromosome Count and Subdivision of the Genus *Cyclamen*

		Number of chromosomes	Karyogram
1.	Subgenus *Psilanthum*		
	1. *C. repandum*	2n – 20	2(ABCDE)
	var. *peloponnes*		
	var. *rhodense* (syn. *C. rhodium*)		
	2. *C. balearicum*	2n – 20	
	3. *C. creticum*	2n – 22	2(ABCDE) + A
2.	Subgenus *Gyrophoebe*		
(a)	Series *Pubipedia*		
	4. *C. coum*	2n – 30	3(ABCDE)
	var. *caucasicum*	2n – 30	
	5. *C. trochopteranthum*	2n – 30	
	6. *C. parviflorum*	2n – 30	
	7. *C. cilicium*	2n – 30	
	var. *intaminatum*		
(b)	Series *Corticata*		
	8. *C. pseudibericum*	2n – 30	
	9. *C. libanoticum*	2n – 30	
	10. *C. cyprium*	2n – 30	
	11. *C. mirabile*	2n – 30	
3.	Subgenus *Eucosme*		
	12. *C. persicum*	2n – 48	4(AABCDE)
	13. *C. rohlfsianum*	2n – 96	8(AABCDE)
	14. *C. graecum*	2n – 84	7(AABCDE)
4.	Subgenus *Cyclamen* L.		
	15. *C. purpurascens*	2n – 34	ABCDE – 2(AABCDE)
	var. *fatrense*		
	var. *colchicum* (syn. *C. colchicum*)		
	16. *C. hederifolium* (syn. *neapolitanum*)	2n – 34	ABCDE – 2(AABCDE)
	17. *C. africanum*	2n – 34	ABCDE – 2(AABCDE)
	18. *C. commutatum*	2n – 68	2(ABCDE) – 2(AABCDE)

Source: Meikle (1979), Schwarz (1964) and Ward (1980).

Twenty-two breeders from seven countries submitted persicum plants and it was found that there was a considerable overlap of cultivars, due to the fact that propagation by cross-pollination causes variation, since cyclamen are mostly grown from seed and not propagated vegetatively. (It is comparatively easy to obtain cultivars from propagated cuttings in other types of plants.)

A large number of the plants were tetraploid with a chromosome number of about 96. The tetraploid cultivars were all German, whereas the English and Dutch varieties had either 48 or 96 chromosomes. The diploid and tetraploid plants were morphologically indistinguishable and most of the cultivars from all the countries were tetraploid, therefore it was concluded that the early mutations of *persicum* from which modern cultivars originally sprang were tetraploid plants.

The fact that hybridisation between the species is impossible in most cases, rare between species with the same chromosome count and difficult between some plants of the same species, may be unwelcome news to the breeder of florists' strains of *persicum* who wishes to introduce characteristics of other species into his stock, but it is promising for the conservationist. It is more likely that the genus will remain essentially unchanged for a longer period of time if the species are not easily altered.

There has been a hold-up in the experiments between species where known crosses have occurred i.e., *balearicum* x *repandum* and *africanum* x *hederifolium*. This has been due to the difficulty of overcoming the natural dormancy period that follows the formation of the seed-leaf. It has been impossible to get the seedlings to continue to mature without a resting period. The cultivated strains of *persicum* will grow on without a break in the right temperature and atmosphere; but it is noticeable that the wild species *persicum* take considerably longer to develop — even if grown in the same environment as the cultivated varieties. Once a way is found to combat this natural obstacle to early maturity, breeding other species besides *persicum* will become a better proposition for the nurseryman interested in the financial prospects.

In the meantime, breeding work on the species *persicum* continues. Some of the novelties are self-sterile. For example, the double-flowering strain has stamens which have become adapted to serve as petals, which means that a proportion of the single-flowering offspring have to be retained so that their pollen can be used on the stigmas of the plants with double flowers. Sterility can also be a side effect of interbreeding when a strain with a particularly attractive characteristic is being built up. Another problem that occurs is fasciation. This involves the deformity of the flower, which never unfolds properly, but remains tightly curled downwards from the tips of the corolla lobes, making the affected flower look rather like a hat with a rolled brim. It is a peculiarity which is seen in the ruffled varieties. At present, the striped, double, fringed, frilled, waved and ruffled varieties have a small but steady following; but if the cut flower side of the trade develops, this is likely to grow. In any case, new types of bloom will always have a certain novelty appeal.

Figure 6.2
C. persicum,
Ruffled Variety

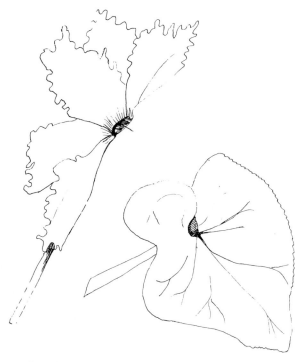

There has been a move in the market in favour of the F_1 hybrids. These are cultivated by crossing two known pure-bred plants and the offspring are referred to as the F_1 generation. Note that the cross can be repeated again and again to produce similar offspring; but if the offspring of the F_1 generation are used for breeding their offspring will be the F_2 generation and will not necessarily all be like their parents or each other. The earliness, the vigour and the uniformity in flowering time makes the F_1 hybrids attractive to growers. The rows and rows of bright scarlet shades in the glasshouses of Holland and Germany are an impressive sight. There can be no doubt that this is a favourite colour on the continent. The German varieties are outstanding for uniformity, perhaps because a quality control and seed certification scheme exists in Germany. A similar organisation, The General Netherlands Inspection Service for Ornamental Plants, controls the raising of cyclamen seed-plants in Holland.

110

Besides the growing popularity of the F_1 hybrids, there is a trend towards the miniature *persicum* plants. The smaller pot-sizes have proved to be more useful. They take less space on the bench and less compost per pot, therefore they are more economical to the grower, and are more attractive to the public than some larger varieties.

The breeders of *Cyclamen persicum* are concerned with raising plants which have qualities that appeal to the public. These include: good, clear flower colours in a wide range of shades, neat foliage — marbled or silvered with intricate patterns, strong stems that are less likely to flop, fragrance, early-maturing and greater resistance to pests and disease. The preference for individual colours influences the market. Apparently, when dark furnishings are in fashion, light-coloured flowers sell well, and when light-coloured furnishings are popular, plants with dark flowers are in demand. The larger seed-firms have a feedback system of information from their customers. The latest requirements are for varieties that perform best during each season of the year. For example, 'Bengali' the popular bright-red hybrid is recommended for November and December, whereas the orchid-mauve variety 'Polka' is earlier maturing and stands flowering at a higher temperature, which makes it suitable for the August/September market. Temperature could be an important factor in certain varieties for flowering quality.

Plant Breeding at Home

The marketing period for cyclamen is extending. Once the trade flourished mostly around Christmas time, but now sales continue from August until April or May. It is possible to have flowering plants on the market throughout the year, but not, however, the popular varieties. There has been a trend towards smaller flowers in recent years. Since 1950, the sales of small pot-plants generally have increased, and attention has been slowly turning to the mini-*C. persicum*. There has been a steady upward growth in the number of miniature plants produced every year. Rochfords alone marketed more than a quarter of a million mini-cyclamen in 1980.

In the flower trials, the judges are looking for quality in the existing stock. Strong flower stems can make a difference to plants that already have other good features such as clear flower colour and compact leaves. There is not much scent in any of the new large-flowering F_1 hybrids, but some of the latest miniature hybrids are quite delightfully fragrant.

There is nothing, except time and sufficient space and equipment, to stop any gardener from commencing a breeding programme of cyclamen. Many of the new varieties that come on to the market have been raised by amateurs.

There is no mystery about artificial pollination — one of our most distinguished hybridisers still uses a camel-hair brush! Unless self-pollination of a special plant is required, the stamens may be removed, and this should be done immediately the flower opens. Take fresh pollen of one flower having the desired features to another newly opened flower. Afterwards, protect the pollinated flowers from insects by covering them with a small piece of muslin or nylon cloth. Check regularly to see if the pedicel has remained turgid, as this will indicate that pollination was successful.

Every breeding programme begins with simple experimental crosses. To make a start, look for a plant that takes your fancy — whether it is silver foliage, a special shade of flower, a particularly strong fragrance, or unusual shape — then couple this with another plant that has good features, such as the required size, vigour and earliness of flowering. With a lot of luck, an interesting plant might occur in the first filial generation.

Most likely, a number of crosses will have to be attempted before worthwhile results are obtained. Records are essential in any breeding programme. A note of every cross with any unusual detail will simplify the task of selecting suitable parents for back-crosses in future.

Now that the time between sowing and first flowering has been drastically reduced, breeding a new variety need not take as many years as in the past. Flowers develop in the same year as the seed is sown; the capsules ripening by mid-summer the following year, or even earlier in some of the mini-varieties. Any interesting leaf forms that show up among the offspring can be marked for future observation. Even at this early stage, it will not be too soon for individual labelling of promising shades of green and shapes. The excitement of finding a good one has somehow to be contained, and the energy harnessed by the knowledge that it is not just a matter of producing an extraordinary specimen, but maintaining outstanding points in a breeding line that comes true from seed. The thrill for the gardener is in raising a new flower that has never been seen before. In cyclamen there are plenty of possibilities and many colours are not yet in existence. Occasionally a mutant colour or petal shape occurs and causes a sensation in the gardening world. The most promising offspring of the F_1 (first filial) generation are sometimes crossed back to either parent with the aim of stabilising excellent features.

C. persicum does not cross with other species and the creation of new varieties is limited to hybridisation between cultivated forms and wild *persicum*, or between cultivated varieties already in existence with the possibility of mutation or 'sports' occurring.

However, since crosses have been recorded between *creticum* and *repandum* and *balearicum* and *repandum*, hybridisers are almost certainly going to continue working on these species, probably with the aim of producing a hardier species for cooler climates without losing the delicate charm of *creticum*. Horticulturalists might also consider the possibility of an all-the-year type flowering variety of the hardy, evergreen *purpurascens*. This fragrant species has been known to bloom perpetually.

Breeding Choice Forms of C. coum

The most treasured forms of *coum* with brightly silvered leaves are self-sterile. The pollen is non-existent or non-fertile. However, if the silvered forms are used as the mother plants and pollinated by other forms of the same species, a variety of silver leaf patterns will be among the offspring. The plain-leaf *coum* is homozygous for foliage colour and never produces silver-leaf offspring. Among the silver-leaf heterozygous offspring will be plants with heart-shaped or kidney-shaped leaves.

Cultivated Varieties of C. hederifolium

These have been raised at a plant-breeding station near Dresden. One variety is packeted and sold as 'Perlenteppich' ('Carpet of Pearls') and the other is called 'Rosenteppich' ('Carpet of Roses'). If names help to sell new varieties then these should be successful.

Pure-breeding varieties have probably come about quite naturally in gardens, simply because they are often isolated in small colonies. Some lovely white-flowering forms exist and some of the pink-flowering plants are beautifully scented.

Annotated List of Strains and Cultivars of *Cyclamen persicum*

Apple Blossom. A popular and successful variety introduced in 1948. Delicate pink flowers.

Aida. Dark salmon-red flowers. F_1 hybrid.

Baby Charm. Holland. Open-pollinated variety raised by Z.K. Tvrtkovic-Sahin.

Bambi. A miniature variety. White with dark eye. Small attractive leaves.

Barbarossa. German. Cristata type of corolla with crested petals. Raised by C. Stoldt.

Bengali. A recent introduction — the brightest scarlet F_1 hybrid yet. A profusion of medium-sized flowers. Thin stems.

Belle Helene. Miniature variety. Many blooms on one plant. Early-flowering. Some plants are scented. Salmon-coloured; but other colours are being developed.

Boheme. An F_1 hybrid with a musical name. This variety has reddish-purple flowers with strong stems. Attractive.

Cardinal. One of the first early-maturing cerise-scarlet varieties to be bred. Suitable for small pots; although not a mini-cyclamen.

Carmen. Scarlet F_1 hybrid. Slightly marbled dark green foliage. Sends up a mass of bloom; but not so free-flowering as 'Bengali'. Tremendous vigour.

Columba. F_1 hybrid. Pale pink with deep red eye; extra compact foliage and strong flower stems. (See also 'Firmament'.)

Cristata Bush Hill Pioneer (1885). An early form which has feathery raised cells on the corolla lobes. Rather a deformed appearance.

Decora. A strain which includes many of the flower colours — fuchsia-pink, salmon, rose and mauve-lilac. Dark centre to the leaves.

De Troyer. Belgium. Extremely bright silver margins are characteristic of this strain.

Firmament series. F_1 hybrids with large flowers and strong growing habit. 'Phoenix' is a bold, clear pink and perhaps the best of this series which includes: 'Columba', 'Orion', 'Pavo' and 'Virgo'. Raised by Messrs Royal Sluis.

Flamingo (1929). Salmon-red with light margin. Raised by Braukmann.

Fragrance Mixed. Open-pollinated cultivars raised by Mr J.T. Fisher.

Fringed cyclamen. These are very popular in Germany, where they are sold in most of the variety colours, both as pot-plants and as cut flowers. Colours include: dark and light salmon, light salmon with a deeper-coloured eye, orchid mauve with dark eye, dark red, pure white, white with carmine eye, scarlet.

Gold Medal Strain (Aalsmeer). This mixture includes: 'Baardse's Wonder' (1938), 'Bonfire', 'Cattleya' — orchid mauve, 'Maarse's Purple', 'Magnificum', 'Pearl of Zehlendorf' (1907), 'Rose of Aalsmeer', 'Rose of Marienthal', 'Scarlet', 'Victoria' and 'White'.

Grandia. A variety with highly ornamental crinkled and ruffled flowers arranged in a half-moon shape against the top of the stem.

Grandiflorum Fimbriatum. A fringed form which first appeared in 1897.

Harlequin. (See 'Striata')

Hallo. Germany. Rich red flowers. Raised by Messrs Ernst Benary Ltd.

Hallo Rex. Variegated foliage form of above.

Kimona. Japan. A cultivar with double flowers raised by Y. Sakata in the 1960s.

Korfu. Germany. This new variety has small, scented flowers and dainty leaves. Salmon-coloured blooms. Introduced by R. Mayer.

Merry Widow. A slightly fragrant white F_1 hybrid with medium-sized flowers. Early maturing; but not such a pure white as 'Swan Lake' or 'Pastourelle'. Raised by Messrs Sluis & Groot.

Monarch. Strains of large-flowering cyclamen marketed by Hurst which include the following — all with the Monarch prefix:

'Apple Blossom', 'Cerise', 'Crimson', 'Excelsior', 'Lilac', 'Mauve Beauty', 'Pink Pearl' (1945), 'Royal Rose', 'Salmon Scarlet', 'Scarlet King' and 'White'.

Nabucco. Light salmon-pink. Large-flowering F_1 hybrid with the typical dark sinus. Matures early which is advantageous.

Oberon. New purple F_1 hybrid — on the paler side of lilac. 'Tosca' is the dark lilac variety in the 1982 Multiflora F_1 hybrid series.

Olympia. Germany. Fringed series suitable for pot-plant culture or cut flowers.

Orion. Pink-flowering F_1 hybrid with good, strong stems and uniform development. (See also 'Firmament')

Pastel Cyclamen. Many were introduced during the 1960s. 'Bach' — deep pink, 'Beethoven' — violet, or dark lilac, 'Brahms' — Cattleya (orchid-mauve), 'Haydn' — Salmon-pink, 'Liszt' — white with crimson, 'Ravel' — dark salmon, 'Schubert' — fuchsia-pink, 'Strauss' — scarlet and 'Wagner' — red and white.

Pastourelle. A blue-white F_1 hybrid from France. Flowers rather full-blown when open. Faintly fragrant. Dark green foliage makes a well-shaped pot-plant. Raised by Messrs. L. Clause S.A.

Pavo. F_1 hybrid. Salmon-pink with deep purple eye. (See also 'Firmament')

Phoenix. F_1 hybrid. Brilliant pink. (See also 'Firmament').

Pink Ruffles. An outstanding variety of German origin. The flowers are a carmine-rose shade of vivid pink with frilly margins. The foliage is also attractive with a hastate pattern of dots on a dark green background and reddish petioles. Altogether one of the best ruffled cyclamen.

Polka. Pretty orchid-mauve flowers appear early in the autumn season. A french F_1 hybrid with lightly marbled foliage.

Puck. French. A mini-cyclamen strain with oval-shaped corolla lobes. Flower colours include: pink, red, lavender, white and bicoloured carmine/white.

Puppet. A miniature strain from Suttons. Small flowers on strong stems. Fragrant. Wide colour range. Very neat foliage. Some plants have intricate silver patterns on the leaves.

Rex. Strain which has light green variegated leaves.

Rheingaufeuer. Germany. Special new variety with pedicels 40 cm in length. The bright-red flowers are held on strong stems high above compact foliage. Medium-sized leaves. Well-shaped blooms suitable for cut-flower arrangements.

Rochfords strain. 'Alpine violets'. Good colour range and nicely shaped blooms. Compact plants with small leaves; known as mini-cyclamen. Last well in the home.

Rokoko. Belgium. A heavily fringed and pleated strain. Popular on the continent as a cut flower.

Rondo. Light rose-pink flowers of medium size appear very early in the season on this French F_1 hybrid.

Rosa van Zehlendorf. Second highest top-selling variety in Holland.

Rosemarie. A variety bred by Professor Wellensiek of the Netherlands. Rose-coloured blooms with a deeper eye.

Rosamunde. Very prolific variety from Holland. Flowers a striking fuchsia-pink — very bright. No fragrance. Long strong stems make this a popular choice. One of the first F_1 hybrids to be introduced, it has become a model of the standard for judging this type of cyclamen. Very early maturing — April sowings are ready for the Christmas market. Raised by Messrs. Sluis & Groot.

Sara. Another variety from Professor Wellensiek. Bright rose flowers.

Scentsation (1977). Strain with fragrant blooms. Flowers not so uniform in size, shape and colour as some of the F_1 hybrids, but rose, salmon, crimson, (no white) are included in the range. Introduced by Hursts.

Silberstrahl. A successful cultivar from Germany, sometimes known in Britain and America as 'Silver Lining'. Dark crimson-red petals with a narrow silver-white line around the margins. Other colours with light-coloured margins are being bred — some waved and frilly.

Silver Cloud. (1977). A mixture introduced by Hurst. Giant blooms and large leaves with wide silver margins.

Silver Lustre. Britain. A strain which includes 'Dawn,' 'Rose', 'Salmon' and 'Scarlet'. Flower colours come true from seed and are sold separately. Silver foliage. 'Dawn Lustre' received an Award of Merit at the Wisley trials, 1979. Raised by Mr J.T. Fisher.

Sonja. A miniature hybrid from Professor Wellensiek. White with a coloured eye.

Figure 6.3 'Striata' or 'Harlequin'

Striata ('Harlequin'). The striped corolla has been in cultivation since the turn of the century. Small but steady sales. The variety will probably remain a mere novelty.

X ½

Swan Lake. A modern F_1 hybrid. Small to medium flowers on long stems. Good foliage. Early maturing. Popular choice. Raised by Messrs. Sluis & Groot.

Sylphe Cattleya. This attractive hybrid with the name of an orchid has lavender flowers with long, slightly twisted corolla lobes, rather like the wild *C.persicum* forms.

Symphony. A mixture of F_1 hybrids from Holland. Large flowers in a good range of colours which include: deep purple, salmon, pale pink, scarlet.

Tosca. Deep rich, lilac-coloured flowers. Distinctive purple eye. F_1 hybrid variety.

Triumph. Strain marketed by Suttons for many years. The colours have individual names: 'Shell-pink', 'Salmon-pink', 'Scarlet', 'Firebrand' (bright-scarlet), 'Crimson', 'Hydrangea-pink', 'Mauve Queen'. 'White Triumph' gained a RHS Award of Merit (1973).

Tzigane. A free-flowering cherry-red F_1 hybrid with the same early, strong-stemmed flowers as 'Rosamunde' and 'Swan Lake'. Showed uniformity in the size of bloom and colour at the trials during 1981-2.

Valiant. Britain. A strain of open-pollinated cyclamen with large, self-coloured flowers that breed sufficiently true to colour for sale in separate seed packets labelled: 'Huntsman', 'Charm', 'Pink Waves', 'Rose', 'Salmon', 'Sunrise', 'White' — all with the 'Valiant' prefix. Marbled foliage. Raised by Mr. J.T. Fisher.

Victoria (1900). This is one of the best-known and most easily recognised cultivars. Spectacular large white corollas with crimson sinus and frilly crimson tips of petals. Fringed margins. The variety is not as difficult to grow as it might seem.

Virgo. White slightly fragrant flowers with strong dark stems that contrast well with the flowers. Leaves without much silver or marbling. Not such a pure white as 'Pastourelle', but makes an excellent large-flowering gift-plant. (See also Firmament)

Vuurbaak. The most popular Aalsmeer Giant type of variety in the Netherlands. The production of seeds and young plants of this orange-red cultivar far exceeds all others in Holland.

Wye College hybrids. British. Strains of miniature cyclamen with distinctive elongated flower petals like the wild forms. Highly scented. Plants with flower colours which breed true to colour have been named after butterflies: 'Wye Downland' — white (no fragrance), 'Admiral' — orchid-mauve, 'Peacock' —pinky/red, 'Fritillary' — dark-red. Dainty, attractive flowers in jewel colours.

CHAPTER 7

Pests and Diseases

Aphids. Fortunately, greenfly and blackfly do not seem to favour the hardy cyclamen. However, greenfly are troublesome in the greenhouse and if they are not removed before the flowers open, petals folding back over rapidly increasing colonies will render them much more difficult to reach, either with sprays or by hand. It is a good idea, therefore, to make a final check for greenfly just before the buds unfold and before plants are taken indoors. However, avoid spraying flowers in full bloom, as you may inadvertently kill pollinating insects or damage the beauty of the petals. Small colonies of greenfly can be washed off houseplant cyclamen with care, or where a number of cyclamen are grown they can be treated with derris, diazinon, malathion or nicotine. Commercial growers of *Cyclamen persicum* regularly use long-term systemic sprays.

Caterpillars. The Cabbage White butterfly, although causing no damage herself, has been known to lay her eggs in the soil around cyclamen. When they hatch, the caterpillars crawl on to the leaves to feed, and later they curl the leaves during the pupa stage. Regular removal by hand of caterpillars and curled leaves is sufficient, as they are not a serious pest of cyclamen. Alternatively, commercial insecticides are effective in killing caterpillars.

Cyclamen Mites (Tarsonemus pallidus) are so small that they are difficult to observe without a hand lens. Plants showing symptoms have distorted new leaves and the petals either have a crippled appearance or the buds do not develop into flowers. As mites spread from plant to plant by crawling between the pots on the shelf, one way of preventing further damage from this pest is to space cyclamen pots as wide apart on the bench as practicable, and pick off deformed buds or leaves as routine procedure. It is best to isolate any new stock for two weeks while carefully examining the foliage at frequent intervals

118

to make sure that it is healthy. Additional control can be obtained by applying Aldicarp granules when potting; or by spraying with dicofol tetradifon solutions and repeating the operation at weekly intervals until the greenhouse is clear of the pest.

Mice. A surprising amount of damage can be done overnight by field-mice. They take the buds from flowers, nipping them off at the top and leaving the pedicels in place. The fact that the stems are left indicates a mouse attack and not another pest or disease. However, in the greenhouse, when mice are hungry, besides buds, petioles might be bitten through, and seedlings, young tubers and leaves are sometimes eaten. Rather strangely, fully opened flowers are not attacked. It appears that only the young growth is damaged and even this only at times of the year when the mice are very hungry. Severe infestations may have to be controlled by the use of mousetraps.

Rabbits, fortunately, do not seem to find cyclamen palatable. However, netting for patches where rare plants are grown is generally recommended by gardeners, although it is not strictly necessary in the case of cyclamen.

Red spider (Tetranychus urticae). This tiny mite favours a hot, dry atmosphere. Therefore, some form of shading during sunny seasons helps to prevent attacks. The leaves look dusty yellow, and the dot-like spider-mites move about mostly on the undersides of the leaves. At two-weekly intervals spray affected plants with derris, malathion or diazinon preparations. Alternatively, gardeners who prefer to use biological control measures in their greenhouses can use another mite (*Phytoseiulus persimilis*) which feeds on the red spiders.

Sciarid-fly. The adult flies are harmless; but the larvae, which look like tiny worms in the compost, eat the roots of cyclamen causing plants to collapse. Water pots with a malathion solution.

Slugs and snails cause terrible trouble. They can be controlled by careful attention to hygiene and by the old-fashioned method of trapping with half an orange placed cut surface down. Slugs don't like creeping across the rough surface of grit used around pots or as a top-dressing, so this is another way of deterring them. But commercial firms may have to resort to slug pellets. These should always be used with care, however, as there is a danger that they might lead to the death of pets and wildlife, which might pick up either the pellets or the poisoned slugs.

Thrips. These little winged insects cause weakening of plant tissues.

119

Damage first shows as yellow speckles on leaves and brownish dots on petals. Derris or malathion sprays used as soon as the first fly is seen, and repeated a week later, will prevent the greenhouse from becoming infested with thrips.

Vine Weevils. The common vine weevil found on cyclamen (*Otiorhynchus sulcatus*) is black with fine yellow speckles on its wing cases; the clay-coloured weevil (*O.singularis*) is brown with lighter freckles on its wing-cases, and (*O.clavipes*), a black, red-legged weevil exists in the limestone districts of the Midlands and south of England. But the species that concerns us here is the cyclamen vine weevil, which is found out-of-doors and under glass. The adult beetles are about 9 mm in length, and it is possible to find them hiding under the rims of pots or in debris during the day. Obviously if greenhouses and growing areas are kept clean, this is the best way to prevent the pest from becoming established. New pot plants brought into the home or nursery should be thoroughly examined for beetles and grubs. The beetles can be knocked off the leaves, but a tuber infested with larvae will have to be discarded. Commercial holdings incorporate an insecticide in the plant compost as a precaution, although the recommended control chemical, Aldrin, is not available to amateur gardeners. Applying diluted gamma-HCH through a slanting hole made with a pencil to reach under the tuber, and also watering over the top of the soil, is a method of getting rid of the grubs.

White Fly (Trialeurodes vaporariorum) is dreaded by most gardeners, but it is not one of the serious pests of cyclamen. The little moth-like flies are conspicuous because of their white colour, although they may not be noticed until several appear from their resting places when a pot is moved. Spray with Lindane, malathion or derris insecticides at weekly intervals until the greenhouse is clear.

Diseases

A major difference between the prevention and treatment of pests and diseases is that with diseases the gardener usually has to wait until symptoms are apparent before attacking the source of the trouble. Research is being carried out regarding the possibility of obtaining one fungus to consume another. However, there is still much work to be done before nurserymen are able to benefit from the results of experiments. In the meantime, keeping the greenhouse clean by clearing away all rubbish and rotting foliage will go a long way towards preventing disease.

Cucumber Mosaic Virus is sometimes transmitted to cyclamen by aphids, but it is not encountered by all gardeners. Control aphids

120

by regular spraying and burn any virus-infected plants.

Damping Off and Root Rots. Use only sterilised potting composts to stop fungus species from building up in the soil. Crowded seedlings and too wet undrained compost favours the fungus. No trouble should occur with sterilised well-drained compost. However, water with Cheshunt compound or captan to check mild attacks.

Fusarium oxysporum. The potting compost must be free from damaging cyclamen wilts such as the *Fusarium* fungus. The best way to control this disease is to use only sterilised soil when potting house-plants, and take care to buy healthy stock. Destroy infected cyclamen and thoroughly clean all containers and equipment. Hardy cyclamen are not usually affected. When purchasing cultivated varieties of *Cyclamen persicum* avoid plants where many of the lower leaves are shrivelled although still green. In your own collection, the odd leaf that shrivels with age, or one leaf that turns yellow as it nears the resting time, is normal.

Grey Mould (Botrytis cinerea). This fungus, which appears as a greyish-brown 'fur' around soft flower stems and petioles, is the most common disease of cyclamen. Fresh air is the best way to prevent it, so have the greenhouse windows and ventilators open and raise the lid or lights on bulb frames whenever the temperature is above freezing. Secondly, during the winter, avoid watering pots from above and certainly avoid watering over the tuber (rain on the hardiest species will not harm them). Otherwise, spray with Rovral or Benlate at the first sign of infection.

Physiological Damage. A special note is included for those who think that they have a diseased plant, when in fact the trouble is due to mismanagement. Cyclamen sometimes begin to go yellow when they are over-watered for long periods. Alternatively, plants that are left dry until all the stems flop down around the pot may look sick, even though they simply need watering. Careful attention to water requirements will result in healthy plants with plenty of foliage and flowers. However, a specimen that has already begun to shed its leaves due to over-watering can sometimes be saved if no more water is given until the top of the compost begins to dry. Also check that the pot and the type of soil used allow for efficient drainage. Plants which have wilted due to lack of water can usually be revived by standing them in a deep saucer or bowl of tepid water for a couple of hours. This is probably the best way to water houseplant cyclamen in the winter, i.e. wait until the compost has almost dried out (but not until the leaves actually wilt) and then water from below. Expert gardeners can water cyclamen from the top throughout the year, as they know exactly when water is required, but even they take care to avoid watering the top of the tuber during cold weather.

CHAPTER EIGHT

Showing Cyclamen

Preparing for
Local Shows

There are numerous small horticultural societies and flower clubs all over the country, and they hold shows which attract thousands of visitors every year. Some local societies have more than one show a year — the largest event is usually arranged in summer, with smaller shows at Easter and harvest-time. Most of them would be delighted to welcome a new member.

Initially, you might prefer to visit a show without actually entering a plant. It will give you an idea of the standard, and you might be encouraged to enter next time. If you do decide to show one of your cyclamen, you will need to obtain, from the show secretary, details of the various classes in the schedule. Not all shows have separate classes for cyclamen, and you might, for example, have to enter your cyclamen in the alpine or houseplant classes.

When selecting cyclamen for the show, choose plants which, although nearly in full bloom, still have buds to come. The flowers and the foliage should be as perfect as possible. Rare species may be shown just for their foliage, but even these will be more interesting if a flower or two is present. Visitors to local shows always seem to go for bright colours or plants with exquisitely dainty blooms. Cyclamen species come into the latter category.

Attention to potting can make all the difference between gaining first and second prize. Hardy cyclamen catch the judge's eye if the tops of the pots are dressed with chippings or tiny pebbles. The pot should always be in proportion to the size of the plant, as an over-potted specimen looks clumsy and a plant in a pot which is too small appears top-heavy. Dirty, unwashed containers, or pots covered in moss, do not help to earn prizes!

Florists' strains of cyclamen may be entered for flower arrangement classes, in horticultural classes as pot-plants, or as cut flowers judged as single blooms. *C.persicum* make excellent show plants as the colours attract the crowds and each individual bloom stays fresh

123

for a considerable time. They are comparatively easy to bring to the right state of development with buds unfolding: the plants can be held back or brought forward a few days by altering the date that they are carried into the house from the greenhouse.

Pick off any obviously yellow leaves or faded flowers. A gentle tug to remove the bloom or leaf complete with pedicel or petiole is best. Dust the leaves or wash them with a damp cloth, but beware of using any form of oil to give a shine, as this might clog the surface cells and damage the foliage. Commercial leaf-shine products may be used with care on the upper surface only; but this has not been found necessary, as clean water is quite sufficient for bringing out the natural shine of the species.

Species cyclamen may also be entered for alpine plant classes in general shows, although if several members wish to enter plants, the committee might consider a special class just for the genus *Cyclamen*. Similarly, where there are no separate classes, florists' cyclamen may be entered in houseplant classes at small shows.

Figure 8.1
A Semi-double
Crested Flower

When travelling to a local show with an entry, if not actually driving, it is best to hold a single plant on your knee; otherwise make sure the precious specimen is fairly well wedged in the boot of the car in case of a sudden jolt. When you reach the show, don't be too shy to ask about how to arrange the plant on the bench, or, in the case of cut flowers, the correct method of making the stems stand up straight in the exhibition vase (by stuffing the container with newspaper!). Other gardeners are pleased to offer help to a novice, and will advise you regarding the merits of individual flowers and leaves, the points that judges look for, or reject, and of course stories of people and plants. You can learn a great deal from conversations at shows.

X ½

Preparing for
Large Shows

Whereas a small local show is a one-day affair, the large national shows are spectacular events with thousands of plants on exhibition. Specialist firms set up stands several days before large shows open to the public.

In London, the Royal Horticultural Society holds regular two-day shows at Westminster every few weeks throughout the year. The Cyclamen Society has a stand at three of these shows — in February, September and November (the September Show lasts three days) and The Alpine Garden Society arranges a competition in spring and autumn.

The standard is high at national shows; therefore it is necessary to prepare entries well in advance. Weeks or months before the show date, choice plants will have to be selected for special treatment and generally pampered; although it should be noted that hardy plants

124

can often be spoiled by coddling.

The stand is generally organised by the show secretary and/or the society team. The display will probably be set up the evening before the show opens to the public, and all the plants should be delivered in time. Remember that if an early start has to be made when taking plants long distances to shows, then everything must be ready the night before. This means not only having pots clean, watered and labelled, but boxed up and ready for the road. The plants should also be suitably housed for the night: an unexpected torrent of rain can wreck cyclamen, or at least mean that most of the pots have to be rehandled. Leaving final preparations until the same day might mean late arrival and this is understandably infuriating for the show secretary.

At the Show

In the case of one-day events, once plants are on the bench, little will need to be done by the owner, other than pick up the pots at the end of the afternoon. If you are unable to remain at the show, be sure to note the closing time. At a two- or three-day show, it will also be necessary to water plants upon arrival, especially after a long journey, as three days without water in a dry, warm hall can have a detrimental effect on cyclamen. This is exaggerated if the compost is on the dry side at the start. Where a group display contains numerous pots embedded in peat, making individual watering difficult, if not impossible, the show secretary will probably ask whoever is attending the stand to spray the plants with water first thing in the morning. The Cyclamen Society takes great care of plants which are lent for exhibition.

Make sure all exhibits are correctly labelled with the species and the form or variety. It is also helpful to the public if the country of origin is added, if this is known. And the owner's initials should be written on the pot - somewhere inconspicuous, if the pot is to be visible and not buried in peat. This is a safeguard against someone removing the wrong plant by mistake, when clearing up at the end of the show. Of course, no initials are permitted on plants entered for competitions.

Judging

A good judge will be an experienced cyclamen grower, who has probably won many first prizes at shows. At national level, it is usual to have more than one judge for each cyclamen class; it is generally agreed that this is the way to eliminate individual preferences and produce an unbiased evaluation. However, one person is usually asked to judge the cyclamen classes at small, local shows, where it is not possible to have two judges for one genus. In every case, the judges will be working on the following criteria.

The judges will decide which species would be the most difficult to grow. When considering the overall excellence of both foliage and flowers, they will look for unmarked, perfectly formed, blooms with no bleached petals, and well-shaped leaves without curl or discolouration. In particular, notice will be made as to whether foliage has been even in growth: a plant that has received a check will carry two different types of leaves; the most obvious sign of this is that one set of leaves appears to have a distinct pattern or other characteristics of the variety, and another set — on the same plant — consists of smaller leaves of a brighter green without the typical markings of the variety. A plant that has many flowers in full bloom with buds still to open will be graded high. However, a species or form that is extremely rare or difficult to cultivate should not be penalised if the flowers are not so plentiful. Quality should be given preference to quantity. Comparing large-flowering cultivars with small-flowering hybrids is not favoured by judges, as it is easier to come to a fair assessment, if separate classes can be arranged.

Tubers should be sound, and where exposed, free from blemish. Attention to presentation, type and size of container, might be taken into account where two or more plants are of equal merit. Otherwise, pots or pans should be as clean as possible, allowing for the fact that some will contain hardy species, grown outside without cover.

Stewards are sometimes appointed to assist the judges. Their job is to make sure the classes are according to schedule (e.g., that plants are not in over-sized pots in classes where the width or height of container is specified) and to check that all cards are placed face downwards on the bench, so that names of competitors are anonymous until after judging, when they are turned over and appropriate prize-colours distributed.

After the Show

It is only when you have shown a number of plants at many different kinds of shows that the importance of after-care is fully realised.

Quite obviously the gardener should be waiting to pick up plants when the show is over and the final bell rung, since less confusion and loss of rare specimens will result. When pots are buried, it is surprising how alike cyclamen can look. Another tip is to carefully remove any surplus peat from the tops of the pots, as this can cause rotting to petioles when plants return home to a change of temperature. Hardy cyclamen definitely seem to be more easily preserved from moulds, moss and even pests such as slugs, if they are given a top dressing of grit.

Specialists with highly prized and possibly valuable — sometimes irreplaceable — plants, might also wish to take the extra precaution of spraying against pests after returning from a show. Yet others might decide it is worth putting them into a quarantine frame. Precautions against pests and diseases can be much simpler than treating them. But don't let this put you off showing your plants. since no-one has complained to the Society of losing cyclamen this way.

CHAPTER NINE

Growing Cyclamen for Commercial Purposes

On a Plant Stall

Besides being sold in shops and garden centres, cyclamen are offered for sale on market stalls, and on plant stalls at local horticultural society shows.

One of the problems of selling cyclamen in the open is that many plants will be in full flower and at their best during the winter months. However, a crop can be raised just for the peak period from November to Christmas by sowing early-maturing mini-varieties in February. The plants should then begin to come into bloom by the first week in November. The hard frosts usually set in around New Year, so after Christmas, tender species such as *persicum* should not be exposed to all weather on an open stall, although the keen grower might turn his attention to the hardy species. Small pots of *coum* look most attractive in bloom throughout the cold months. Under cover, pots of *persicum* will sell well on a stall from autumn until Easter, with Christmas as the peak selling period — the bright colours of the flowers drawing potential customers to the stall on dull winter days.

Figure 9.1
C.coum

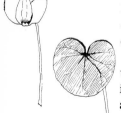

Cyclamen of all kinds will be very welcome on the 'plant stall' table at local horticultural shows and flower arrangers' club meetings: some societies hold regular monthly gatherings. Other clubs and societies, e.g. women's clubs, also have horticultural interests and demonstrations of the art of flower arrangement and pot plant displays. At any of these, plants are frequently set out on a table for members to buy at bargain prices. Whenever cyclamen appear, they are always the first plants to be sold and a percentage of the purchase price can be donated to help club funds.

A number of seedlings can quite easily be raised economically for this purpose, if advantage is taken of the summer months for growing on young plants, in order to save on expensive winter heating costs. Arrange your sowing programme so that a number of young plants — possibly the surplus to your own requirements — are ready whenever a space on a sales table needs filling. Young plants may be offered at the spring and summer shows; plants with buds about to open at the harvest show, and others in full bloom at the AGM, which usually takes place in winter.

If you are able to help your local society by supplying a quantity of cyclamen for sale, it is best to let the secretary know in advance. Some societies are glad to provide small pots (also donated) for members who are prepared to grow plants especially for selling at shows. Take your cyclamen for the stall to the venue when you take your plants for exhibition, although make sure your show stock is arranged before turning your attention to the sales table, as the 'all out' bell that warns people that judging is about to commence, is usually rung at about 11 o'clock. It is surprising how much there is to do on the mornings of show days.

For Charity

The gardener who has surplus seedlings, but who does not want to open his garden to the public or sell plants commercially, can always help a charity. It can give an added incentive to grow some of the new varieties, or more of the less common forms —, and great pleasure can be gained by spreading the joy of gardening to others. Anyone who has taken a tray of young plants to a charity stall knows how enthusiastically they are received. Free seedlings offered to an audience after a talk are taken up by many eager hands; sometimes people come back and ask for more information.

These are good reasons for *giving* plants away for charity. But there are many organisations where garden products are sold for charity. Sometimes the gardener donates growing plants or seedlings with the understanding that the money raised will go towards helping a particular charity. Occasionally, by arrangement, a percentage of the purchase price goes to charity and the remainder to the grower.

The Cyclamen Society is a registered charity and welcomes seed, seedlings, young plants or mature tubers for sale at shows and Open Days. Plant material may be donated, or an agreed percentage of the money given to the Society. The secretary will be pleased to send further details to anyone, although a stamped, addressed envelope would be appreciated (see Useful Addresses). All money gained in this and other ways, on behalf of the Society, goes to help conserve the species in the wild; and to help spread knowledge of the genus and improve growing methods of plants in cultivation.

Commercially — Through the Post

Crocuses, daffodils, hyacinths and tulips are widely grown in fully mechanised nurseries and thousands of bulbs come on to the market every year. The tender houseplant cyclamen are also produced in large quantities in America, Britain, Germany and Holland. However,

129

the breeding of new varieties is still in the hands of amateur gardeners; and the production of hardy cyclamen is almost entirely by small, specialist nurseries, where a great deal of time is devoted to maintaining healthy stock and building a reputation for reliable service. The success of this type of nursery depends on keeping customers satisfied that the plants are of the highest standard.

One of the advantages of growing species cyclamen for sale is the fact that they can be grown continuously in pots. In mild areas, some of the species can also be naturalised and used as stock plants for seed; the seedlings being potted and later sold. In areas where it is possible to grow the semi-hardy species outside, cloches may be used to protect the foliage from heavy rain during early spring. However, the majority of the plants in a cyclamen specialist's nursery are best housed in an alpine house. A bulb frame can also be used to hold the overflow of container-grown mature plants of the more common species. Much attention should be given to daily inspections of plants. Routine work will consist obviously of sowing, potting and keeping the plants free from weeds and moulds. Pests and diseases should not cause too many losses. Cyclamen are fairly resistant to disease if they are well-grown and there are few pests that cause serious trouble. These can be avoided by preventative measures, or controlled with careful use of chemicals.

Cyclamen in flower attract their own customers and established garden centres should have little difficulty in selling a range of small pots of hardy cyclamen in bloom. The species *hederifolium* and *cilicium* can be raised from seed to flowering-size in two years and many of the other species will come into flower within three years from sowing.

Gardens which are situated a long way from a main road or a large town might make excellent places to grow rare bulbs; but there is a problem for the would-be nurseryman: customers may be more difficult to find in a remote spot. One way to overcome this is to send plants to customers by post although this will necessitate extra labour and materials for packing. In the early years, nurserymen send out a simple list, whilst building up stocks of plants and the goodwill of their customers. Then as demand for more varieties and rare forms grows, the list develops into a full catalogue.

Specialist nurserymen sometimes advertise their stock in garden journals; others rely on satisfied customers passing on the news that they received correctly labelled, healthy, well-packed plants. It is not always possible to reply by return of post; but plants must be dispatched promptly once they are packed, since cyclamen plants deteriorate if they are kept without air for many days. The wrapping has to be light to keep postage (especially air-travel) costs down, yet the coverings should give some protection against crushing, and the

130

roots should be moist, as the plants will suffer a check if they become dry.

Gibberellic acid, a hormone derived from a fungus, generally speeds up growth; but so far it has not been found a commerically viable proposition for increasing flower stem length, for earliness of flowering, or for use on seedlings. Further research is needed.

CHAPTER TEN

Cyclamen and the Artist

Painting

In the eighteenth and nineteenth centuries, descriptions of plants in gardening catalogues and botanical magazines were accompanied by a drawing made by, or under the supervision of, a botanist. Curtis's *Botanical Magazine* was an early arrival, and it is the longest surviving periodical: founded in 1787 and still published today. The colour-print drawings are extremely fine in the early volumes. In Vol. I, there is a detailed portrait of *Cyclamen coum* showing carmine flowers, a coiled capsule, kidney-shaped leaves, a dark brown tuber and pale, sepia-coloured, fibrous roots. The date on the plate is 1786. In Vol. II, Wiliam Curtis has included a delicate drawing of a white form of *C. persicum*.

Comparing these paintings of cyclamen with the work done in the sixteenth century, we can see that although artists have always had individual styles, as unique and recognisable as handwriting, the method of reproduction has changed over the years. In 1576, the herbalist, Matthias de l'Obel, used simple woodcuts to illustrate *Plantarum seu stirpium icones*. He included a picture of the species *C. hederifolium*, labelled *Cyclamen folio Hederae* (T718). It is interesting that exactly the same woodcut picture appears in *The Herball* by John Gerard, which was published in London in 1597. (In his section on *Cyclamen* in the Turkish Flora (1978), Mr Meikle comments that *C. hederifolium* is 'probably best typified by the plate in Gerard's Herball'.)

In 1861, *The Floral Magazine*, 'comprising figures and descriptions of popular garden flowers' by Thomas Moore, Secretary to the Floral Committee of the RHS, includes a large coloured drawing of pink and white *persicum* in a bold, simple style by Walter Fitch. Even at this date the species could be described as the 'old Persian Cyclamen'. The fragrant forms were highly praised, as they are now. However, Moore wrote: 'This quality can only be determined when the seedlings reach a blooming state.' And, all these years later, we still have difficulties getting strains that will breed true for fragrance. Pictures in the magazine between 1867 and 1870 include paintings of *persicum* flowers which have been picked from more than one variety to show contrasting colours, and arranged against brightly marbled leaves.

William Robinson was editor of *The Garden* between 1868 and 1912. His most famous book *The English Flower Garden* was published during this period in 1883. Gertrude Jekyll, who was five years younger than him, published *Colour in the Flower Garden* in 1908 — without coloured drawings! Botanical pictures were mostly hand-coloured until 1948 and black and white illustrations of flowers were usually reproduced by a printing method known as lithography. Paxton's *Flower Garden* came out during the year of the Great Exhibition, in 1851, and the pictures were hand-painted at that time, but coloured by machine-print for the issue of 1873.

There are numerous hand-painted pictures of cyclamen carefully preserved by horticultural libraries. Nowadays, of course, paintings of flowers in books and magazines are reproduced by modern complex printing techniques, which involve colour photography.

Botanical paintings are regularly exhibited at the first and last Shows of the RHS in the New Hall, Greycoat Street, Westminster, London. It is well worth a visit to see the work of artists who have painted flowers and subjects related to horticulture and botany.

It is hoped that anyone who grows cyclamen, or admires the species **Poetry** in the wild, will also enjoy reading poetry — at least for the pleasure of seeing the varying impressions that this alpine plant made on the poets.

> St. John's wort and fresh Cyclamen
> She in his chamber kept,
> From the power of the evil angels
> To guard him while he slept.

> (Old Ballad)

Many poems on flowers were published in Victorian times. These lines from an American poem are undated, but they come from a delightful old book, entitled *Poetry of the Flowers*, 1801-1864, selected by Mrs C.M. Kirtland.

> *The Sweet-scented Cyclamen*

> I love thee well, my dainty flower
> My wee, white cowering thing,

That shrinketh like a cottage maid,
Of bold, uncivil eyes afraid,
　Within they leafy ring!

I love thee well, my dainty dear!
　Not only that thou'rt fair, —
Not only for thy downcast eye,
Nor thy sweet breath, so lovingly,
　That woos the caller air.

But that a world of dreamy thoughts
　The sight of thee doth bring.
Like birds who've wandered far from hence
And come again (we know not whence),
　At the first call of Spring.

As here I stand and look on thee,
　Before mine eyes doth pass —
(Clearing and quick'ning as I gaze,)
An evening scene of other days,
　As in a magic glass.

(Mrs Southey)

In a book of poetry entitled: *'A Victorian Anthology' 1837-1895* (which has a picture of Queen Victoria as a frontispiece) there are a number of poems by Walter Savage Landor (1775-1864). He inherited a fortune and lived on the continent, spending a lot of time in Italy during the last fifty years of his life. Besides the five volumes of verse which he published in the English language, he also wrote poetry in Latin. His poetry shows that he was interested in flowers and natural phenomena. Other titles include: 'Cowslips', 'Three Roses', and 'There are Sweet Flowers'.

To a Cyclamen

I come to visit thee agen,
My little flowerless cyclamen;
To touch the hand, almost to press,
That cheer'd thee in thy loneliness.
What could thy careful guardian find
Of thee in form, of me in mind,
What is there in us rich or rare,
To make us claim a moment's care?
Unworthy to be so carest,
We are but withering leaves at best.

(Published in 1846; reprinted 1858, 1876, 1895.I. 'again' 'agen' 1858)

Ezra Pound (1885-1972) spent his first twenty-three years in America. He is one of the most purely aesthetic poets of the twentieth century. But his poems are also didactic and concerned with 'the basic needs of the human spirit; real wealth as a spiritual harvest of love, worked for celestially, ritualistically, agriculturally, politically and personally in every walk of life.'[1] He wrote a poem entitled 'The Spring' in which cyclamen appear in these lines:

> O bewildered heart,
> Though every branch have back what last year lost,
> She, who moved here amid the cyclamen,
> Moves only now a clinging tenuous ghost.

D.H. Lawrence (1885-1930) wrote 'The first change in scene comes when for the first time I left Nottinghamshire, at the age of twenty-three, to go to teach in a new school on the fringes of South London. From the playground we could look north at the blue bubble of the Crystal Palace, fairy-like to me.'[2] Many years later in the autumn of 1920 in Tuscany, he began the poems of 'Birds, Beasts and Flowers'. In the long poem 'Sicilian Cyclamens', Lawrence is telling us about cyclamen, greyhounds, toads, mud, hares and Sicily, while at the same time writing on mankind and dawn light. Here is an extract:

> Dawn-rose
> Sub-delighted, stone-engendered
> Cyclamens, young cyclamens
> Arching
> Waking, pricking their ears
> Like delicate very-young greyhound bitches
> Half-yawning at the open, inexperienced
> Vista of day,
> Folding back their soundless petalled ears.
> Greyhound bitches
> Bending their rosy muzzles pensive down,
> And breathing soft, unwilling to wake to the new day
> Yet sub-delighted.

References

1. *The Concise Encyclopedia of English and American poets and poetry*, 1970. Ed. Stephen Spender and Donald Hall, Hutchinson.
2. D.H. Lawrence, *Collected Poems*, 1928 (Reprint 1933) Heinemann.

Cyclamen and the Artist

Photographing cyclamen can be a hobby in itself. Often an interest in photography develops from an interest in gardening and a desire to record a flower, so that others might benefit from the beauty: an attempt to immortalise a moment of perfection.

Growing a plant to near perfection is one skill; learning to use the camera to create an artistic picture is another. The amateur photographer gradually acquires the knowledge needed to arrange the plant at the right angle in a light that will not result in shadows which distract the eye from the subject. The aim is to obtain a picture that shows botanical detail and yet retains that elusive lightness of the cyclamen flower. But it is surprisingly difficult to gain good results, especially when photographing the smaller species and forms. Close-up pictures must still present a pleasing pattern of flower, stem, foliage and coiled capsule blending or contrasting harmoniously with the background; and even parts of the plant showing detail should have a clear outline. Experts will spend a long time arranging a rare plant or a new variety, taking pictures at more than one angle against different backgrounds.

Modern, view-through-the-lens cameras make colour photography easier. The gadgets do most of the work! The artist merely has to select the subject, decide on the background, and consider the pattern made by light and shade. In poor light it might be advisable to use a flash unit. This is also useful for indoor work.

Early gardeners and botanists found it much more difficult to take photographs of their treasured specimens and collections, as a record for albums or educational purposes. Therefore, the achievement of Edward Cohen was considerable. He took hundreds of pictures on glass negatives, many of which have been given to the Royal Horticultural Society. His garden at Bird's Fountain, Dunsford, Nr Exeter, contained a wide range of trees and shrubs. He had many interests besides cyclamen, as the photographs, which include portraits of Sir Henry Wood and Jacob Epstein, indicate. The cyclamen negatives were of the species *cilicium*, *coum*, *hederifolium*, *repandum* and *persicum*, which he called *indicum*. (Dr William T. Stearn discusses this synonym in the Cyclamen Society's Journal (Vol. III, No. 1). Most probably Linnaeus's *C. indicum* was based on a cyclamen with abnormal flowers.) There are close-ups of individual flowers, a plant of *cilicium* spread out to show the botanical features, and views of naturalised cyclamen.

Raising special plants can take years, so it is worth spending a little time on the photography. A few minutes devoted to arranging the flowers and foliage with an eye to colour combination and overall design might make the difference between a record of a jumble of shapes, or clear outlines of isolated petals and single well-defined leaves. The pattern of light and shadow is as important as the colours and forms.

Botanists and horticulturalists will look for detail, the artist hopes for more: detail linked to overall design and harmony of everything in the picture. Occasionally, the most poetic photograph comes by chance from, perhaps, an ever so slightly out of focus flower, which seems to catch a certain light.

Glossary

Acid soil   Soil or compost with a pH below 7.0.

Alkaline soil   Soil of compost with a pH above 7.0

Alpine plant   A plant which in nature grows between the treeline and the permanent snowline on mountains.

Anther   The pollen-bearing top part of the stamen.

Bulb   Food storage organ. Strictly speaking, cyclamen have swollen hypercotyles, although they are often included in lists of bulbous plants.

Capsule   The dry fruits or seed-bearing organs.

Chromosome   The body in the cell nucleus bearing the genes, which contain the hereditary factors.

Classification   The arrangement of plants (and animals or things) into an order, so that each kind is grouped with others of the same sort. Plant species are grouped into a genus.

Clone   Plant which is identical to another obtained by vegetative propagation from a single plant or cell.

Corolla   The coloured part of the flower consisting of the petals, which are fused at the base in cyclamen.

Cotyledon   The first seed-leaf that appears after germination. In the case of cyclamen a second cotyledon usually emerges if the first is damaged. Two seedling leaves rarely appear together from the seed.

Cultivar   A cultivated variety which has distinguishing characteristics, and which can be reproduced without losing those characteristics.

Diploid   Having two sets of chromosomes.

Eye   A term sometimes applied to the white or pink centre of the flower.

F_1 hybrid   The first filial generation.

Fasciation   Deformity of the leaves or flowers.

Fimbriated   In cyclamen, flowers with fringed margins.

138

Genus   A group of species with common characteristics. For example, all cyclamen belong to the genus *Cyclamen*, all saxifrages to the genus *Saxifraga*, etc.

Heterozygous   Where two genes of a pair are different an organism is said to be heterozygous for a particular character.

Homozygous   Where two genes of a pair are identical an organism is said to be homozygous for a particular character.

Karyotype   A set of chromosomes prepared for study.

Mutant   A plant displaying a different characteristic from its ancestors. Mutants occur spontaneously and are sometimes referred to as 'sports'.

Parthenogenesis   A form of reproduction where the unfertilised ovum develops into a seed.

Pedicel   The flower stem.

Petiole   The leaf stem.

Pollen   The male cells carried on the anther.

Pollination   Transference of the pollen from the anthers to the stigma.

Resting Period   A dormant period when the plant makes no growth — natural to cyclamen.

Self-colour   A flower of a single uniform colour.

Species   A group of plants with similar characteristics. The term may also be applied to a single plant.

Stamen   The male part of the flower consisting of the anther (with pollen grains) and the filament.

Stigma   The tip of the style, which conveys the pollen to the ovary.

Synonym   An alternative name for a plant.

Style   Part of the flower, extending from the ovaries, which bears the stigma.

Tetraploid   Having four sets of chromosomes.

Tuber   Food storage organ.

Vegetative reproduction   A means of producing new plants from cuttings rather than propagation from seeds.

Useful Addresses

The Cyclamen Society

The Cyclamen Society is still in its infancy — it was founded in 1977 — and it is hoped that the Society will become the International Registration Authority with full responsibility for registration and nomenclature. In due course, it is also hoped that standards for judging exhibition plants will be recognised and adopted. The Society aims to increase the available knowledge of the genus, which will lead to a better appreciation of the need for conservation of plants in the wild. For further information about the Society, please write to:

The Cyclamen Society,
7 Montreal Road,
Ilford,
Essex.
Secretary: Dr Malcolm Summers
Editor: Colonel J.A. Mars

The National Trust

The National Trust,
42 Queen Anne's Gate,
London SW1H 9AS

Nurseries in Britain

Avon Bulbs, Bath, Somerset
Richard Bixby, Hook Lane Nursery, Lambourne End, Essex (cultivated strains of *C.persicum*)
Blackmore & Langdon Ltd., Bath, Avon (cultivars of *C.persicum*)
Broadleigh Gardens, Barr House, Bishops Hull, Taunton, Somerset (hardy *Cyclamen* and miniature bulbs)
P.J. & J.W. Christian, Pentre Cottages, Minera, Wrexham, Clwyd, N. Wales (hardy *Cyclamen* species and alpines)

140

J.T. Fisher, Priest Street, East Markham, Newark, Notts (cultivated strains of *C.persicum*)

W.E.Th. Ingwersen, Birch Farm Nursery, Gravetye, E. Grinstead, Sussex (alpine plants, sink gardens)

Reginald Kaye, Waitham Nurseries, Silverdale, Carnforth, Lancs. (alpines and hardy ferns)

T. Rochford, Turnford Hall, Broxbourne, Herts. (houseplant cyclamen)

Tile Barn Nursery (P. Moore), Standen Street, Iden Green, Benenden, Kent TN17 1JU (hardy and rare *Cyclamen*)

Thuya Nurseries (S. Bond), Glebelands, Hartpury, Glos. (alpines)

Wye College, Commercial Horticultural Dept., Wye, Ashford, Kent TN25 5AH (miniature hybrids of *C.persicum*)

Seeds

Asmer Seeds Ltd, Asmer House, Ash St., Leicester LE5 0DD

Samuel Dobie and Son, Upper Dee Mills, Llangollen, Denbigh, Wales

Hurst Gunson Cooper Taber Ltd, Witham, Essex CM8 2DX

Suttons Seeds Ltd, Hele Road, Torquay, Devon TQ2 7QJ

Thompson & Morgan, London Rd, Ipswich, Suffolk

Societies

Alpine Garden Society, Lye End Link, St John's, Woking, Surrey GU21 1SW

Cyclamen Society, 7 Montreal Rd, Ilford, Essex

National Trust, 42 Queen Anne's Gate, London SW1H 9AS

Northern Horticultural Society, Harlow Car Gardens, Harrogate HG3 1QB

Royal Horticultural Society, The Secretary, Vincent Square, London SW1P 2PE

Woodland Trust, Westgate, Grantham, Lincolnshire NG31 6LL

World Wildlife Fund, Panda House, 29 Greville Street, London EC1N 8AX

Special Project Concerning Growing Hardy Cyclamen Plants:

Sheltered Employment Unit, Fairfield Opportunity Farm, Dilton Marsh, Westbury, Wiltshire

Overseas Addresses

Bamberger Cyclamen, Robert Mayer, 86 Bamberg/Bayern, W.Germany

Wilhelm Beck, Cyclamenzucht, 7430 Metzingen, W.Germany

Gerhard Bubeck, Cyclamen-Spezialkulturen, 7262 Althengstett Kr. Calw, W.Germany

Walter Hammerschmidt & Sohn, 3051 Kolenfeld uber Wunstorf,

W.Germany

Edgar L. Kline, 17495 S.W. Bryant Road, Lake Grove, Oregon 97034, USA

Nichols Garden Nursery, 1190 North Pacific Hwy, Albany, Oregon 97321, USA

Erfurter Samenzucht, Weigelt & Co. 6229 Walluf im Rheingau, W.Germany

C. Stoldt, 2252 St Peter-Ording, Wittendüner Allee 76, W.Germany

Fritz Tangermann, 3204 Nordstemmen I, Heyersumer Str. 21, W.Germany

Ernst Walz, Postfach 30 12 28, D-7000 Stuttgart 30, W.Germany

Cyclamen Seed Producers in Holland

Klaas Visser, Machineweg 206, Aalsmeer

Gebr. Man, Noordammerweg 104a, Amstelveen

Pannevis, Postbus 2, 1600 AA, Enkhuizen

Royal Sluis, P.O. Box 22, 1600AA, Enkhuizen

Bibliography

Bailey, R.H. (ed.) (1978) *Cyclamen Proc. Conf. Cyc. Soc.*, Cyclamen Society

— (1980) *Cyclamen Proc. Conf. Cyc. Soc.*, Cyclamen Society

Botanical Magazine (various issues)

Botanical Register (1827) vol. XIII, t. 1095

Bowles, E.A. (1949) 'Cyclamens in the Garden', *Journal RHS*, vol. 74, p. 325

Davis, P.H. (1956) 'The Spring Flora of the Turkish Riviera', *Journal RHS*, p. 167

— (1965-78) *Flora of Turkey and the East Aegean Islands*, 6 vols., Edinburgh

Doorenbos, J. (1950) 'Taxonomy and Nomenclature of *Cyclamen*', *Meded. Landb. Wageningen*, vol. 50, pp. 17-29

Gerard, J. (1597) *The Herball or General History of Plantes*, London

Hildebrande, F. (1898) 'Die Gattung *Cyclamen* L Eine Systematische und Biologische Monographie', Jena

Journal of the Cyclamen Society (various issues)

Journal of the Royal Horticultural Society (various issues)

Legro, R.A.H. (1959) 'The Cytological Background of *Cyclamen* Breeding', *Meded. Landb. Wageningen*, vol. 59, pp. 1-51

Linnaeus, Carolus (1735) *Systema Naturae*, Stockholm

Loudon, J.C. (1828) *An Encyclopaedia of Gardening*, London

Loudon, Mrs Jane *Loudon's Ladies' Flower Garden*, London

Maatsch, R. (1971) *Cyclamen*, Paul Parey, Berlin/Hamburg (in German)

Meikle, R.D. 'Cyclamen' (1978) *Flora of Turkey* (Ed.) Davis, P.H. Edinburgh

Miller, Philip (1768) *Miller's Gardeners Dictionary*, 8th edition, London

Palmer, L. (1960) 'Cyclamens', *Journal RHS*, vol. 85, pp. 210-17

Palmer L. and Synge, P.M. (1965) 'The Winter-flowering *Cyclamen*', *Journal RHS*, vol. 90, pp. 293-8

Bibliography

Parkinson, J. (1629) *Paradisi in sole paradisus terrestris*, London

Robinson, William *The Wild Garden*, London

Schwarz, O. (1964) 'Systematische Monographie der Gattung *Cyclamen* L.', *Teil II Feddes Reprium Spec. nov. Regni. Veg*, vol. 69, no. 2, pp. 73-103

Saunders, Mrs D.E. (1973) 'Cyclamen. A Gardener's Guide to the Genus', Alpine Garden Society, Woking

Sweet, Robert (1825-7) *British Flower Garden*, vol. II, London

Thompson, William (1852-3) *The English Flower Garden*, London

Wellensiek, S.J. (1955) 'The Genetics of Diploid x Tetraploid and Reciprocal *Cyclamen* Crosses', Publication 135, Laboratorium voor Tuinbouwplantentedt, Landbouwhogesschool, Wageningen, The Netherlands

Index

Page numbers in italics refer to line drawings

Index

Index